RIGBY
star

Planning and Assessment Guide

Yellow, Blue and Green Levels

Renewed Framework Edition

RIGBY

Contents

Welcome to Rigby Star Guided Reading

Rigby Star Guided Reading is designed to help you manage guided reading in your classroom so that every lesson is successful and purposeful. It offers more than 180 fiction and non-fiction guided reading books for Foundation Stage and Key Stage 1, structured in 12 colour-banded levels. There are annotated Teaching Versions of every guided reading book, assessment materials that are easy to use, and follow-up reading and writing activities. Some Rigby Star Guided Reading titles have been written with an emphasis on maximising phonic opportunities.

Structuring learning with Rigby Star

The renewal of the Primary Framework for literacy focuses on the effective teaching of early reading and stresses that it needs to be taught daily using high-quality, engaging texts.

However, teachers face a daily challenge of selecting quality fiction and non-fiction books at the right level for each reading group. They also need to find time to plan every guided reading session and monitor and assess children's reading. Teachers report that guided reading sessions are more successful with books that offer excitement and variety at the right level. In Rigby Star we have tried to address all of these needs and provide a suitable balance of fiction and non-fiction books which ensure that learning is effectively structured over a series of lessons. These books provide opportunities for children to use and apply their developing literacy skills.

Rigby Star Guided Reading books

The Rigby Star fiction books are individually designed to bring the excitement and pleasure that children find in picture books and big books into guided reading. Each book has a named author and illustrator, a real story with a satisfying ending and lavish illustrations. Rigby Star covers a range of genres including realistic, fantasy, humorous, rhyming stories, traditional tales and plays.

Features of the Rigby Star non-fiction books designed to develop children's non-fiction reading skills include tables of contents, indexes, glossaries, captions, schematic diagrams, and so on. The books also provide exposure to a range of non-fiction text types, such as instructions, information books, reports and reference books.

Rigby Star also has a rigorous structure: there is a progression in phonic skills, common (high frequency) words are gradually introduced and language structures become more complex through the programme so that children become confident, motivated, multi-skilled readers.

The right book for the right child at the right time

For a young child it is intensely exciting to be a real reader, provided the first reading of a new book is successful. The texts in Rigby Star have been carefully levelled to ensure children meet books at the right level at the right time. Rigby Star levels have been correlated to The Reading Recovery National Network guidelines in *Book Bands** and to National Curriculum English Reading SATs levels.

* *You can order Book Bands from* The Reading Recovery National Network, Institute of Education, 20 Bedford Way, London WC1H 0AL.

Help with planning and running lessons

Rigby Star Guided Reading provides an annotated Teaching Version of every book. The Teaching Version includes a guided reading lesson with details on how to introduce the book, questions to ask during the session, and suggestions for follow-up work. The Teaching Versions help you plan and run guided reading lessons. Each Teaching Version links to reading objectives in the renewed Framework and focuses on the appropriate word recognition and language comprehension skills. The Teaching Version can also be used by a classroom assistant to run additional follow-up guided reading sessions. Further information about the Teaching Versions can be found on page 10 of this guide.

Clear objectives for each lesson

Rigby Star links to the renewed Primary Framework for literacy, offering coverage of the following reading strands of learning:

- Strand 5: Word recognition: decoding (reading) and encoding (spelling)
- Strand 7: Understanding and interpreting texts
- Strand 8: Engaging with and responding to texts

While the reading strand 6 (Word structure and spelling) is not treated explicitly as a guided reading learning objective, you will find opportunities to develop children's spelling in the Rigby Star follow-up work.

Charts summarising the teaching objectives of each book are given on pages 20–47 of this guide. The charts are organised by Book Band level and then by 'type' (fiction/phonic opportunity/non-fiction).

For a chart showing the full details of the Primary National Strategy's 12 strands of learning for literacy (Year One), please see page 185 of this guide.

Rigby Star and the simple view of reading

The renewed Framework recommends the adoption of a new conceptual framework called 'the simple view of reading'. The simple view of reading outlines two dimensions to reading: word recognition (learning to read) and language comprehension (reading to learn). High-quality phonics teaching secures the crucial skills of word recognition which help children develop high level language comprehension skills.

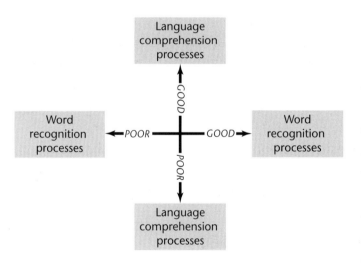

The diagram illustrates how both word recognition and language comprehension processes are necessary for reading, but neither is sufficient on its own. If children cannot recognise the words on the page, they cannot fully understand the text; however, recognising and understanding the words on the page is no guarantee that the text will be understood. Rigby Star provides opportunities for both processes to be developed during guided reading lessons. The Teaching Versions for each book highlight clearly the opportunities for both processes, ensuring that your children become secure in recognising words **and** develop comprehension skills. For more information on how the Teaching Versions help to support you with the simple view of reading, see page 10 of this guide.

Rigby Star and writing

Each guided reading book is accompanied by a photocopy master of a writing activity to be used by children in independent group activities. The photocopy masters can be used in a guided writing context with those children who need the support of an adult. Alternatively, they can be used by more advanced groups, working independently.

Components Chart

Yellow level

Yellow

Blue level

Blue

Green level

Green

Phonics

Non-fiction

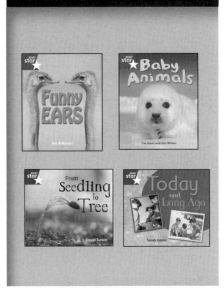

Every title has its own Teaching Version

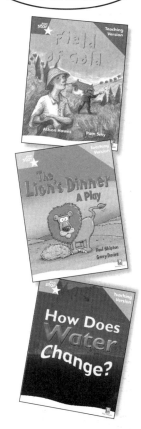

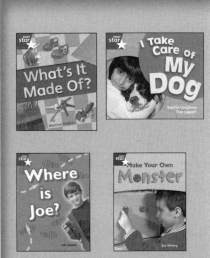

Planning and Assessment Guide

Lilac, Pink, Red Levels
– *see Foundation Stage Planning and Assessment Guide*

Orange, Turquoise, Purple, Gold, White and Lime Levels
– *see Year Two Planning and Assessment Guide*

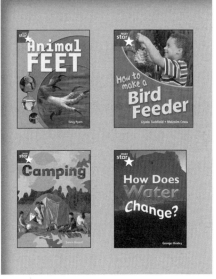

How to use Rigby Star Guided Reading

 How children progress through the programme

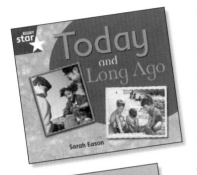

Rigby Star has been graded in colour-banded levels. Within each level there is a carefully graded progression of books. The Rigby Star Guided Reading fiction books may be read in a progressive way following the order on pages 6–7 of this guide. Some children may not need to read every book in every level, particularly if the texts and level are providing minimal challenge for them. Rigby Star provides guidance to enable you to place individual children at an appropriate level and book of Rigby Star.

Some children will need opportunities to re-visit guided reading texts they have already read, to consolidate what they have learned. These familiar texts can be kept in browsing boxes for independent 'reinforcement reading'.

 How to begin using Rigby Star

When you begin using Rigby Star you will need to place children in groups according to their reading ability. The Assessment section on pages 48–54 of this guide together with your own knowledge of your children will help you place them in groups and decide where they should begin the programme.

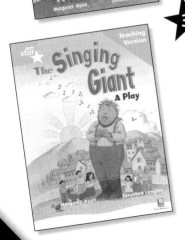 **How Rigby Star helps you plan and teach each guided reading lesson**

A guided reading lesson works well when there is a clear teaching focus. Each Rigby Star Guided Reading book has one or two main teaching objectives. There is a Teaching Version for each book that helps you plan and run a focused guided reading lesson. The Teaching Versions include full teaching notes for each book.

⭐ 4 How Rigby Star provides follow-up work for reading and writing

Each Teaching Version contains suggestions for follow up group and independent work. In addition, this guide provides two photocopiable activities per book. One photocopy master focuses on reading, and the other focuses on writing. At the back of this guide there is an index which lists all the photocopy masters in the sequence in which they appear (see pages 183–184).

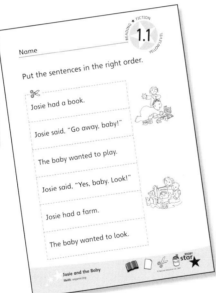

⭐ 5 How Rigby Star helps you to monitor and assess progress

You can use the Rigby Star assessment materials to place children in your class on an appropriate level of Rigby Star and in suitable ability groups. The week before half term is a good time to carry out re-assessments and re-group children if necessary. There are other times when adjustments need to be made. Some children may make sudden progress or begin to struggle within their group. When this happens you can use the assessment materials to put these children on an appropriate level of Rigby Star and to re-arrange the groups.

Planning a guided reading lesson

Guided reading lessons work best when the teacher is familiar with the text and has a clear focus for the lesson.

Rigby Star Teaching Versions are designed to save you hours of planning and preparation time. Each one provides the complete guided reading book, annotated with information to help you run a guided reading lesson. The back cover of each Teaching Version includes information you need for planning the guided reading lesson.

Familiarisation with the text

Rigby Star provides a range of stories, with predictable structures and patterned language, and simple non-fiction texts and recounts, which reflect the experiences of Year One children. The back cover of the Teaching Version gives the genre of the story and a summary to enable you to quickly familiarise yourself with the book.

A clear teaching focus

It is important to have clear teaching objective/s for each guided reading lesson. This provides a focus for your teaching, enables you to monitor what the children are learning and helps link assessment to your teaching objectives.

On the back of each Teaching Version you will find the suggested teaching objective/s for that book linked to the reading strands of learning in the renewed Framework. The objective/s are organised so as to support you with the simple view of reading; distinguishing between the word recognition objective and the language comprehension objective.

Every guided reading book from Pink to Green level has two teaching objectives that are the focus of the guided reading lesson in the accompanying Teaching Version: one objective linked to word recognition skills (strand 5) and one objective linked to language comprehension skills (strands 7 or 8).

At Lilac level, the six fiction guided reading books have one teaching objective linked to language comprehension skills (strands 7 or 8). These are wordless books, with an emphasis on understanding how a book works. The remaining two fiction books (with phonic opportunities), have two teaching objectives: one linked to word recognition skills (strand 5) – exploring sounds and links to letters – and one linked to language comprehension skills (strands 7 or 8).

Every guided reading book from Orange to Lime level has one teaching objective linked to language comprehension skills (strands 7 or 8) with guidance on consolidating the children's growing word recognition skills.

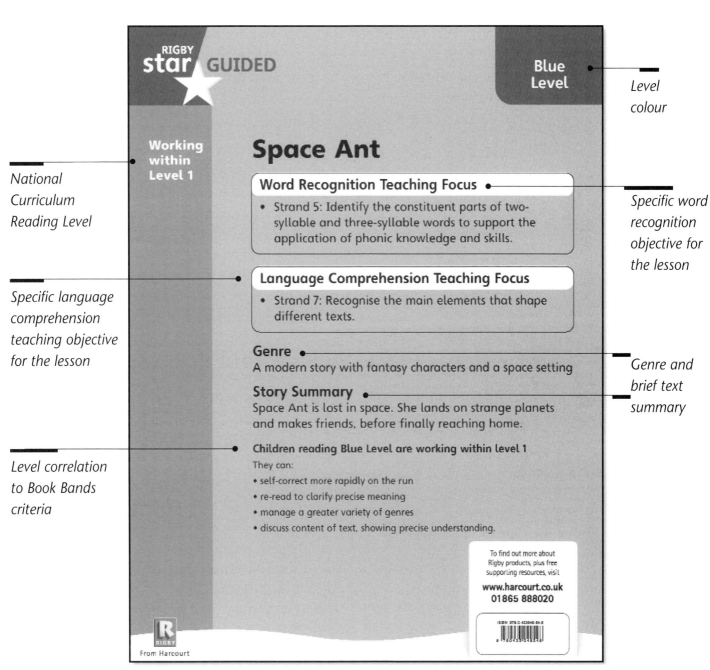

National Curriculum Reading Level

Specific language comprehension teaching objective for the lesson

Level correlation to Book Bands criteria

RIGBY **star** GUIDED

Blue Level

Level colour

Working within Level 1

Space Ant

Word Recognition Teaching Focus

• Strand 5: Identify the constituent parts of two-syllable and three-syllable words to support the application of phonic knowledge and skills.

Language Comprehension Teaching Focus

• Strand 7: Recognise the main elements that shape different texts.

Genre
A modern story with fantasy characters and a space setting

Story Summary
Space Ant is lost in space. She lands on strange planets and makes friends, before finally reaching home.

Children reading Blue Level are working within level 1
They can:
• self-correct more rapidly on the run
• re-read to clarify precise meaning
• manage a greater variety of genres
• discuss content of text, showing precise understanding.

To find out more about Rigby products, plus free supporting resources, visit

**www.harcourt.co.uk
01865 888020**

ISBN 978-0-433048-54-8

R RIGBY
From Harcourt

Specific word recognition objective for the lesson

Genre and brief text summary

Back cover of Rigby Star Teaching Version Space Ant

Running a guided reading lesson

In a guided reading lesson, a group of six children each have a copy of the same book. The book has been selected to match the group's ability so that some features offer a manageable challenge to the children. The children hold and read their own copy of the book. They read it in a quiet voice independently during the guided reading lesson while the teacher observes and monitors each child's reading.

A guided reading lesson consists of three parts: a teacher-led preparation for the child's independent reading of the book; the child's independent reading of the book; and a review of the child's independent reading.

The Rigby Star Teaching Versions are structured to support each part of the guided reading lesson. On the inside front cover of each Teaching Version you will find suggestions for: how to use the Walkthrough (which is called Tuning In in the non-fiction titles) to prepare children for their first reading of the text; how to use the Observe and Prompt section to monitor children during their first reading of the text; and how to use the Revisit and Respond section to carry out follow-up work after the children's reading. There are also assessment points for each book to help you evaluate whether the children have understood the teaching objective/s of that book.

Before a guided reading lesson

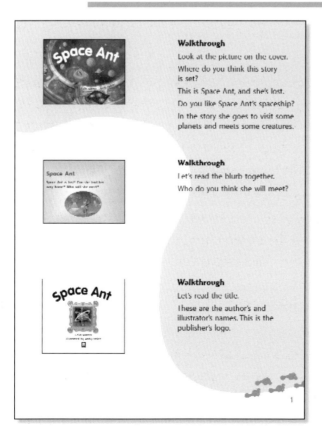

Rigby Star Teaching Version of Space Ant

The teacher begins the lesson by sharing the teaching objectives with the group (see back cover of the Teaching Version). This is presented in language that the children can understand so that they know what the focus of their learning will be, e.g. 'We are learning to notice the type of setting and the characters in this story, and to discuss what makes a fantasy story.'

Book orientation

The first part of the Walkthrough is the book orientation. Using the front cover as a focus the teacher gives a brief summary of the story. The orientation is designed to capture the children's interest and alert them to anything in the text which might be new or challenging.

The Walkthrough/Tuning In

The Walkthrough (or Tuning In in non-fiction titles) prepares each child for an independent reading of the text. The Walkthrough is designed to unlock the text for the children prior to reading so that when they come to read it for themselves they can do so with minimal support. The teacher takes the children through the whole book focusing on the illustrations and photographs. While the children enjoy the pictures, the teacher draws their attention to significant aspects of the story or narrative.

There may be opportunities to draw children's attention to special features such as speech bubbles. Prediction is an important element in reading and children may be asked for their ideas about what might come next. Where appropriate, the teacher may look at features of non-fiction texts, introducing the new ideas.

The teacher briefly summarises the key reading skills that the children will need to use in this lesson. This skill check reminds children of the particular reading behaviours that they are working on. The teacher may refer to the children's Self-Assessment Sheets and pick out a particular statement that will be useful when they are reading the book. For example, 'Remember that you can repeat a sentence to make the meaning clearer as you notice the speech marks or full stops.'

During a guided reading lesson

Observe and Prompt

After the first part of the guided reading session, the children return to their own copy of the book and read it independently to themselves. Each child in the group should read the whole text in a soft voice at his or her own pace. The children do not read round the group taking turns, as in a 'round robin', but rather work at the text on their own asking for help when needed.

The children should be able to read the text relatively easily by themselves. There will be some features of the text which are new to the children. The teacher should observe how the children try to problem-solve these challenges and offer prompts to help the children problem-solve independently. Assessment is embedded in this part of the lesson as the teacher observes what the children have learnt and can apply independently, and reminds them of the new skills they are learning.

The Rigby Star Teaching Versions include an Observe and Prompt section which offers suggestions to help the teacher foster useful reading behaviours and indicates where a child may need help with problem solving.

At Year One, as the child reads independently, the teacher may prompt him/her to:
– take note of punctuation, grammar, and text features to read with expression
– pay attention to phrasing to clarify precise meaning
– use phonic information to decode unknown words.

The teacher can use questions to make a quick assessment of children's understanding and to check whether individuals can correct their own mistakes. By using questions such as 'You corrected that yourself – how did you know that it was … instead of …?', the teacher can help children appreciate that they are monitoring their own reading for meaning and accuracy.

Walkthrough/Tuning In: Questions which cue the text

Suggestions for prompting children's reading which focus on the word recognition skills they will be using to decode the text

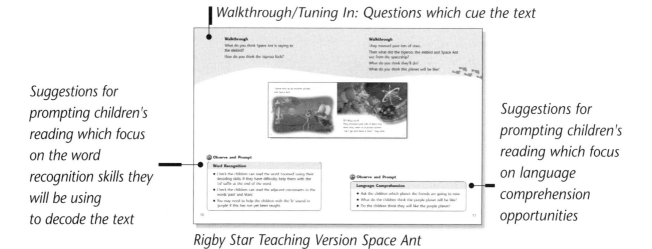

Suggestions for prompting children's reading which focus on language comprehension opportunities

Rigby Star Teaching Version Space Ant

Observe and Prompt: Word Recognition

These suggestions for prompts focus on the skills that children will be using to decode the words on the page. To consolidate your high-quality phonic teaching, the prompts encourage children to use their phonic knowledge, and knowledge of sight words, to decode the text. For example, if a child comes across a new word which has more than one syllable, the prompt may suggest you ask them to break the word down into syllables before blending the whole word together.

Observe and Prompt: Language Comprehension

These suggestions for prompts focus on the language comprehension skills that can be developed during the reading. The suggestions may cover prediction skills, literal comprehension skills, or simply encourage links between the text and the child's personal experiences.

How to use the Observe and Prompt sections

The simple view of reading demonstrates not only how both word recognition and language comprehension processes are crucial to the development of fluent reading, but also how children can vary in their acquisition of these two distinct processes. In this way, you can choose to use both sets of Observe and Prompt suggestions (i.e word recognition and language comprehension) during a guided reading session. Alternatively, you can choose to focus on one set of prompts for a group of children who may need to concentrate on that particular dimension of reading.

After a guided reading lesson

Revisit and Respond

When the children have finished their first reading of the book the teacher may revisit it with the children to explore the book more fully, deepen comprehension and carry out specific teaching.

The Rigby Star Teaching Versions contain Revisit and Respond activities which explore the teaching opportunities that have arisen in the text. They consolidate the main teaching objective/s and offer further suggestions for teaching.

In the final part of the guided reading lesson, the teacher has an opportunity to give oral feedback to the children about their learning. The teacher can give examples of successful problem solving observed during independent reading. The group can reflect on their learning, by referring back to the teaching objectives, and think about how they will be able to use these skills for their wider reading. The teacher talks through any problems that were encountered so that the children understand how they can learn from their mistakes. There may be some discussion of what the children can do as a result of their learning.

The children can make use of their Self-Assessment Sheets (see pages 52–53 for further information) to identify the skills that they used in the lesson. They can go on to think about which skills they need to work on in the future.

Revisit and Respond activities, rounding up the session

Group and independent activities

Assessment points

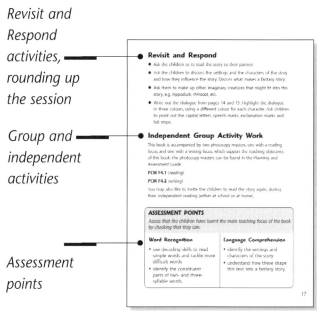

Rigby Star Teaching Version Space Ant

Independent group activity work

After reading the book in a guided reading lesson children may carry out independent group work arising from the book. As previously mentioned, Rigby Star provides two photocopy masters to accompany each book in the programme. One photocopy master has a reading focus, and the other has a writing focus. The Teaching Version refers to the relevant photocopy masters in this Planning and Assessment Guide.

Assessment points

The Rigby Star Teaching Versions include assessment points which you may use to determine whether the children have understood the main teaching objectives of that book. This assessment, along with the children's self-assessment, can inform planning for the group's next guided reading session.

Rigby Star Levels

Rigby Star comprises 12 levels for Foundation Stage and Key Stage 1. There are three levels at Year One: Yellow, Blue and Green. Once early reading behaviours are established, children are eager for a greater challenge. Rigby Star Yellow, Blue and Green level texts retain predictable structures and limited vocabulary supported by illustrations. However, the variety of structures within and across texts gradually increases, and children need to pay greater attention to their own reading in order to monitor the integration of meaning, print and language cues.

Yellow level

The twenty books at Yellow level include realistic stories, with some fantasy tales and two plays. Four of these books have an emphasis on phonic opportunities. There are an additional four non-fiction books at Yellow level.

At Yellow level, children encounter the familiar characters of Curly the Caterpillar and Josie and her friends. They also meet a range of new characters, both children and animals. Many of the realistic stories at Yellow level feature boys as main characters and have themes which will appeal to both boys and girls.

The settings are familiar: home, cinema, dentist, hospital, supermarket, funfair, farmyard, and reflect a young child's everyday experience.

The stories have repetitive phrase patterns with some variation in sentence structure to help children build confidence in early to mid Year One.

The story text presents children with a variety of reading experiences. Some books involve reading signs and notices in context (*Where's My Car?*). There are opportunities to discuss story structure, e.g. days of the week (*What a Week!*) and language features, e.g. alliteration (*Super Shopping*).

The two plays (*Pop!* and *The Lion's Dinner*) offer opportunities for children to take on character roles and enliven their reading. *Pop!* is a play version of a wordless story at Lilac level.

The titles with specific phonic teaching opportunities have been written with familiar and repetitive patterns, enabling children to build and consolidate early phonics skills and to improve the fluency and expression of their reading.

The non-fiction titles give children the opportunity to read simple reports and information books.

The Yellow level fiction books provide opportunities for:

- developing awareness of character and dialogue
- describing settings
- discussing the plot
- relating the story to their own experiences
- comparing story themes
- appreciating key features of the story language
- reading aloud with expression, taking account of punctuation and emboldened text.

The Yellow level non-fiction books then provide opportunities for:

- reading simple reports, noting the non-fiction features
- understanding the purpose of contents and index pages.

In both the fiction and non-fiction books at Yellow level, there are opportunities to recognise word endings such as 'ed' and 's' for plurals, and to discriminate and blend phonemes to read unknown words.

Children working comfortably at Yellow level can cross-check all sources of information. They can follow print with their eyes, finger pointing only at points of difficulty. Their reading reflects spoken language rhythms and they are able to use punctuation to reflect oral language phrasing as they read, in order to bring the story to life.

To assess the progress children are making in Yellow level there is a Reading Behaviour Checklist for Yellow level on page 55 of this guide.

Rigby Star Yellow level Josie and the Baby

Blue level

There are fourteen stories at Blue level, six of which have an emphasis on phonic opportunities. There are an additional four non-fiction books at Blue level.

The themes of the stories deal with feelings, for example fear, rejection, loneliness, bullying, making friends. There are also opportunities for deeper characterisation. The stories provide a range of reading experiences including stories told in rhyme (*Terrible Tiger* and *Mrs Mog's Cats*) and a book featuring word play (*A Ball Called Sam*).

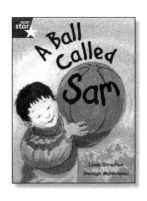

Blue level provides opportunities to compare stories by the same author (*Josie and the Play* and *Josie's New Coat*), and to read stories on similar themes (*Josie and the Play* and the traditional tale *The Ugly Duckling*).

The titles with specific phonic teaching opportunities enable children to continue to develop their focused phonic skills in a range of genres and contexts.

The non-fiction titles give children the opportunity to read simple reports, recounts and instructions and to interpret simple maps.

In addition to the opportunities that the Yellow level offers, the Blue level fiction books provide opportunities for:
- using inference to determine the feelings of characters
- comparing different versions of stories
- reading rhyming stories with appropriate pace and expression
- recognising capital letters for the beginning of names
- identifying thought bubbles and commenting on the part they play in the story and the impact on meaning.

The Blue level non-fiction books then provide opportunities for:
- using the terms fiction and non-fiction
- recognising the structure of recounts
- understanding that not all non-fiction books have to be read from beginning to end
- predicting what a book might be about.

In both the fiction and non-fiction books at Blue level, there are opportunities to recognise contractions and realise the apostrophe replaces the vowel, and to recognise rhyming words in a variety of spelling patterns.

Children reading successfully at Blue level can self-correct as they read, phrasing appropriately to clarify precise meaning.

To assess the progress children are making in Blue level there is a Reading Behaviour Checklist for Blue level on page 56 of this guide.

Green level

There are twelve stories at Green level, four of which have an emphasis on phonic opportunities. There are an additional four non-fiction books at Green level.

The language of the stories at Green level is more literary, the characterisation is more subtle, the plots are more complex and there are opportunities to develop inferential skills.

There is a range of genre: realistic, fantasy, traditional tale and animal fable and one play. *The Singing Giant* is in both story and play form so children can compare two versions of the same story.

The titles with specific phonic teaching opportunities have been written to enable children to continue to develop their focused phonic skills in a range of genres and story settings.

The non-fiction titles give children the opportunity to read simple reports, recounts and instructions.

In addition to the opportunities that the Yellow and Blue levels offer, the Green level fiction books provide opportunities for:
- discussing characters and speculating about reasons for their behaviour
- understanding time and sequential relationships in a story.

The Green level non-fiction books then provide opportunities for:
- identifying simple questions and using text to find answers
- reading and following instructions.

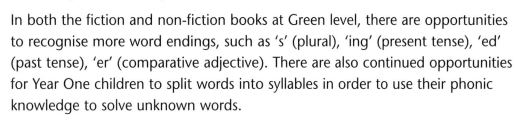

In both the fiction and non-fiction books at Green level, there are opportunities to recognise more word endings, such as 's' (plural), 'ing' (present tense), 'ed' (past tense), 'er' (comparative adjective). There are also continued opportunities for Year One children to split words into syllables in order to use their phonic knowledge to solve unknown words.

Children reading confidently at Green level can read fluently paying attention to punctuation. They can solve new words using their decoding skills while also attending to the meaning and syntax.

To assess the progress children are making in Green level there is a Reading Behaviour Checklist for Green level on page 57 of this guide.

Rigby Star Teaching Objectives

Yellow Level: Fiction

Title	Word Recognition Teaching Objective	Language Comprehension Teaching Objective
Josie and the Baby	• Strand 5: Recognise and use alternative ways of spelling the phonemes already taught, for example, that the long vowel sound 'a' can be spelt with 'ai' and 'ay'.	• Strand 8: Visualise and comment on events, characters and ideas, making imaginative links to their own experiences.
Pop! (A Play)	• Strand 5: Recognise automatically an increasing number of familiar high frequency words.	• Strand 4: Act out stories, using voices for characters.
Grandpa	• Strand 5: Recognise automatically an increasing number of familiar high frequency words.	• Strand 8: Visualise and comment on events, characters and ideas, making imaginative links to their own experiences.
What a Week!	• Strand 5: Identify the constituent parts of two-syllable and three-syllable words to support the application of phonic knowledge and skills.	• Strand 7: Identify the main events and characters in stories.
At Last!	• Strand 5: Recognise automatically an increasing number of familiar high frequency words.	• Strand 7: Make predictions showing an understanding of ideas, events and characters.

• You will find full teaching notes in the Teaching Version for each book.

• For a chart showing you the strand objectives of the renewed Framework, please see page 185 of this guide.

Common Words	Genre	Linked Rigby Star Independent Reader	
away • go had • play said	Modern realistic story with familiar family setting, two characters and patterned language.	Go and Get It!	Skills focus: To relate the story to own experience
all • are look • you	A simple play in a familiar setting with animal characters and friendly interaction.	Look at Me!	Skills focus: Character and dialogue
me • said yes • you	Modern realistic story with a familiar setting, two characters and patterned language in question and answer format.	A Toy for Vik	Skills focus: To relate the story to own experience
	A modern realistic story with a familiar setting and predictable structure based on days of the week.	Too Many Pets	Skills focus: Retelling the main events
at	A modern realistic story using a limited variety of sentence structures.	Hare and Tortoise go to School	Skills focus: Making predictions

Yellow Level: Fiction (continued)

Title	Word Recognition Teaching Objective	Language Comprehension Teaching Objective
The Computer Game	• Strand 5: Recognise and use alternative ways of spelling the phonemes already taught, for example, that the long vowel sound 'a' can be spelt with 'ay' and 'a-e'.	• Strand 7: Use syntax and context when reading for meaning.
Where is Curly?	• Strand 5: Recognise and use alternative ways of pronouncing the graphemes already taught, for example, that the grapheme 's' is pronounced differently in 'said' and 'his'.	• Strand 7: Identify the main events and characters in stories.
Have you got everything, Colin?	• Strand 5: Recognise and use alternative ways of pronouncing the graphemes already taught, e.g. 'c' in 'pencil' and 'case', and 'g' in 'gym' and 'got'.	• Strand 7: Make predictions showing an understanding of ideas, events and characters.
The Lion's Dinner	• Strand 5: Apply phonic knowledge as the prime approach to reading and spelling unfamiliar words that are not completely decodable.	• Strand 4: Act out stories, using voices for characters.
The Dentist	• Strand 5: Read more challenging texts which can be decoded using their acquired phonic knowledge and skills, along with automatic recognition of high frequency words.	• Strand 7: Recognise the main elements that shape different texts.

• You will find full teaching notes in the Teaching Version for each book.

• For a chart showing you the strand objectives of the renewed Framework, please see page 185 of this guide.

Common Words	Genre	Linked Rigby Star Independent Reader	
play • said	A modern realistic story in a familiar setting with a predictable structure.	My Wild Woolly	Skills focus: Recognising alternative spellings
here • where	A fantasy story with familiar characters and setting, and predictable structure.	Where is Little Bo Peep?	Skills focus: Storybook language and rhyme
have • your	A modern realistic story with a predictable structure and some variation in text patterns.	What a Catch!	Skills focus: Understanding characters
do • don't what	A funny play with animal characters, patterned language, and predictable structure.	Mister Wolf's Plan	Skills focus: Characters
look • you	A modern realistic story with a familiar setting and predictable structure.	Josie and the Cake Sale	Skills focus: High frequency words

Title	Word Recognition Teaching Objective	Language Comprehension Teaching Objective
Super Shopping	• Strand 5: Apply phonic knowledge and skills as the prime approach to reading and spelling unfamiliar words that are not completely decodable.	• Strand 7: Explore the effect of patterns of language and repeated words and phrases.
Where's Our Car?	• Strand 5: Read more challenging texts which can be decoded using their acquired phonic knowledge and skills, along with automatic recognition of high frequency words.	• Strand 7: Make predictions showing an understanding of ideas, events and characters.
I Can't Open It!	• Strand 5: Apply phonic knowledge and skills as the prime approach to reading and spelling unfamiliar words that are not completely decodable.	• Strand 7: Make predictions showing an understanding of ideas, events and characters.
Rush Hour	• Strand 5: Read more challenging texts which can be decoded using their acquired phonic knowledge and skills, along with automatic recognition of high frequency words.	• Strand 8: Visualise and comment on events, characters and ideas, making imaginative links to their own experiences.
Curly to the Rescue	• Strand 5: Apply phonic knowledge and skills as the prime approach to reading and spelling unfamiliar words that are not completely decodable.	• Strand 7: Explore the effect of patterns of language and repeated words and phrases
Be Quiet!	• Strand 5: Apply phonic knowledge and skills as the prime approach to reading and spelling unfamiliar words that are not completely decodable.	• Strand 7: Use syntax and context when reading for meaning.

• You will find full teaching notes in the Teaching Version for each book.

• For a chart showing you the strand objectives of the renewed Framework, please see page 185 of this guide

Common Words	Genre	Linked Rigby Star Independent Reader	
first • got • said the	A modern realistic story with familiar setting and predictable structure.	Jen's Brilliant Birthday	Skills focus: Language patterns
look • mum • out said • some • we went	A modern realistic story with a predictable structure and familiar setting.	Clean-Up Day	Skills focus: Decoding challenging words
and • can't • don't he • pull(ed) • said the • then • this went	A modern story with animal characters, a predictable structure and a familiar theme and setting.	Curly and the Big Berry	Skills focus: Applying phonic knowledge: -ed endings
are • dad • I • on said • they	A modern realistic story with familiar setting, variable language pattern and dialogue.	Elvis	Skills focus: Applying phonic knowledge: question words
came • come down • eat • help pull(ed) • said up • will	A fantasy story with a predictable structure and patterned language.	Furball to the Rescue	Skills focus: Reading unfamiliar words
be • everyone got • his	A modern story with a familiar setting and predictable structure.	Quiet in the Library	Skills focus: To read aloud, recognising punctuation

Yellow Level: Phonics

Title	Word Recognition Teaching Objective	Focused Phonic Opportunities
Booooo!	• Strand 5: Recognise and use alternative ways of spelling the phonemes already taught.	• Decoding words with alternative spellings of the short vowel 'e' phoneme as in 'head' and 'next'
Ping-Pong	• Strand 5: Recognise automatically an increasing number of familiar high frequency words.	• Decoding CVCC and CCVC words • Recognising sight words including the days of the week
Josie Helps Out	• Strand 5: Identify the constituent parts of two- and three-syllable words to support the application of phonic knowledge and skills.	• Decoding words with more than one syllable
Bert's Boat	• Strand 5: Recognise and use alternative ways of spelling the phonemes already taught.	• Decoding words with alternative spellings of the long vowel 'o' phoneme as in 'boat', and the 'er' phoneme as in 'Bert'

- You will find full teaching notes in the Teaching Version for each book.
- For a chart showing you the strand objectives of the renewed Framework, please see page 185 of this guid

Language Comprehension Teaching Objective	Common Words	Genre
• Strand 8: Visualise and comment on events, characters and ideas, making imaginative links to own experiences.	all • and • got • have • he his • I • look • said • then you • a • for • my • to • of their	Story with familiar setting
• Strand 7: Identify the main events and characters in stories.	do • I • on • play • up with • a • dog • it • my	Story with repetitive pattern
• Strand 7: Identify the main events and characters in stories.	all • got • on • like dad • they • of	Story with familiar setting
• Strand 7: Make predictions showing an understanding of ideas, events and characters.	and • on • the • this is • it • a	Story with repetitive pattern

Yellow Level: Non-fiction

Title	Word Recognition Teaching Objective	Language Comprehension Teaching Objective
Funny Ears	• Strand 5: Read and spell phonically decodable two-syllable and three-syllable words.	• Strand 7: Find specific information in simple texts.
Baby Animals	• Strand 5: Read more challenging texts which can be decoded using their acquired phonic knowledge and skills, along with automatic recognition of high frequency words.	• Strand 7: Find specific information in simple texts.
From Seedling to Tree	• Strand 5: Identify the constituent parts of two-syllable words to support the application of phonic knowledge and skills.	• Strand 8: Distinguish fiction and non-fiction texts and the different purposes for reading them.
Today and Long Ago	• Strand 5: Identify the constituent parts of two-syllable and three-syllable words to support the application of phonic knowledge and skills.	• Strand 7: Find specific information in simple texts.

• You will find full teaching notes in the Teaching Version for each book.

• For a chart showing you the strand objectives of the renewed Framework, please see page 185 of this guide.

Common Words	Genre	Linked Rigby Star Independent Reader	
has • have these • too where	Report		Skills focus: Using an index
called • too	Simple information		Skills focus: Reading unfamiliar words
called • come did • from • it this • where	Information book	No linked title	
are • do • from how • these this • what which • with your	Report	No linked title	

Blue Level: Fiction

Title	Word Recognition Teaching Objective	Language Comprehension Teaching Objective
A Ball Called Sam	• Strand 5: Read more challenging texts which can be decoded using their acquired phonic knowledge and skills, along with automatic recognition of high frequency words.	• Strand 7: Recognise the main elements that shape different texts.
Josie and the Play	• Strand 5: Apply phonic knowledge as the prime approach to reading and spelling unfamiliar words that are not completely decodable.	• Strand 8: Visualise and comment on events, characters and ideas, making imaginative links to own experiences.
Terrible Tiger	• Strand 5: Recognise and use alternative ways of spelling the phonemes already taught, for example that the long vowel sound /a/ can be spelt with 'ai', 'ay' and 'a-e'.	• Strand 7: Explore the effect of patterns of language and repeated words and phrases.
Space Ant	• Strand 5: Identify the constituent parts of two-syllable and three-syllable words to support the application of phonic knowledge and skills.	• Strand 7: Recognise the main elements that shape different texts.

• You will find full teaching notes in the Teaching Version for each book.

• For a chart showing you the strand objectives of the renewed Framework, please see page 185 of this guide.

Common Words	Genre	Linked Rigby Star Independent Reader	
boy • but • girl little • play then	A modern realistic story with a theme of making friends.		Thematic link: Children at play
away • back be • can • don't school • then want(ed)	A realistic story about putting on a play of the traditional tale, *The Ugly Duckling.* Familiar characters.		Thematic link: The school play
away • bed don't • him his • there	A modern story with rhythm, rhyme and suspense.		Thematic link: Bedtime fears
another • back came • got have • here not • off • out too • then there • with	A modern story with fantasy characters and a space setting.		Thematic link: Colours

Blue Level: Fiction (continued)

Title	Word Recognition Teaching Objective	Language Comprehension Teaching Objective
Bully Bear	• Strand 5: Recognise and use alternative ways of pronouncing the graphemes already taught, for example, that the grapheme 'oo' is pronounced differently in 'Moose' and 'took'.	• Strand 7: Identify the main events and characters in stories.
Josie's New Coat	• Strand 5: Read more challenging texts which can be decoded using their acquired phonic knowledge and skills, along with automatic recognition of high frequency words.	• Strand 7: Identify the main events and characters in stories.
Vroom!	• Strand 5: Apply phonic knowledge and skills as the prime approach to reading and spelling unfamiliar words that are not completely decodable.	• Strand 7: Use syntax and context when reading for meaning.
Mrs Mog's Cats	• Strand 5: Identify the constituent parts of two-syllable words to support the application of phonic knowledge and skills.	• Strand 7: Explore the effect of patterns of language and repeated words and phrases.

• You will find full teaching notes in the Teaching Version for each book.

• For a chart showing you the strand objectives of the renewed Framework, please see page 185 of this guide.

Common Words	Genre	Linked Rigby Star Independent Reader	
can't • has little • new now • saw took	A fantasy story with animal characters and theme of bullying.	Josie and the Bully	Thematic link: Bullying
but • can't have • new saw • same too	A modern realistic story with a predictable structure and simple language.	The New Babysitter	Skills focus: To retell main events
along • came come • down out • that • time very • one • two	A modern story with animal characters and the theme of conservation.	Slurp! Burp!	Thematic link: Animal Journey
be • has • old there	A modern rhyme with patterned language and predictable structure.	I Love Rocks	Thematic link: Rhythm and Rhyme

Blue Level: Phonics

Title	Word Recognition Teaching Objective	Focused Phonic Opportunities
Chicken Licken	• Strand 5: Identify the constituent parts of two-syllable and three-syllable words to support the application of phonic knowledge and skills.	• Using phonic knowledge and skills to decode words with two syllables
Blue Goo	• Strand 5: Recognise and use alternative ways of spelling the phonemes already taught.	• Decoding words (including nonsense words) that use different spellings for the phonemes 'oo' as in 'goo' and 'er' as in 'first'
Curly and the Honey	• Strand 5: Recognise and use alternative ways of spelling the phonemes already taught.	• Decoding words with different spellings of the long vowel 'ee' phoneme

• You will find full teaching notes in the Teaching Version for each book.

• For a chart showing you the strand objectives of the renewed Framework, please see page 185 of this guide.

Language Comprehension Teaching Objective	Common Words	Genre
• Strand 7: Identify the main events and characters in stories.	down • one • then • but • help • I • just must • his • where • way • here • day	Traditional story
• Strand 7: Make predictions showing an understanding of ideas, events and characters.	I • am • going • make • first • some of • will • call(ed) • and • a • now • at time	Fairy story
• Strand 7: Identify the main events and characters in stories.	here • a • little • what • he • see tree • on • the • in • out • come • all very • look • one • two • three	Fantasy story

Blue Level: Phonics (continued)

Title	Word Recognition Teaching Objective	Focused Phonic Opportunities
Field of Gold	• Strand 5: Recognise and use alternative ways of spelling the phonemes already taught.	• Decoding words with different spellings of the long vowel 'ay' phoneme
Super-Duper Shoes	• Strand 5: Recognise and use alternative ways of spelling the phonemes already taught.	• Decoding words with different spellings of the long vowel 'oo' phoneme as in 'shoes'
The Whale in the Well	• Strand 5: Recognise and use alternative ways of spelling the phonemes already taught.	• Decoding words with different spellings of the long vowel 'ow' phoneme as in 'ground' • Decoding words with more than one syllable

• You will find full teaching notes in the Teaching Version for each book.

• For a chart showing you the strand objectives of the renewed Framework, please see page 185 of this guide

Language Comprehension Teaching Objective	Common Words	Genre
• Strand 7: Identify the main events and characters in stories.	an • old • man • so • his • this there • jump(ed) • up • away I • for • will • he • said • in but • you • must • have • again over • as • now	Story from another culture
• Strand 7: Explore the effect of patterns of language and repeated words and phrases.	I • some • for • a • are • an • do when • with • and • on • the no • more • just • have • look	Modern realistic story
• Strand 7: Identify the main events and characters in stories.	was • in • a • and • all • about one • day • there • little • down you • look • come • see • new pull(ed) • could • not • how so • much	Traditional story

Blue Level: Non-fiction

Title	Word Recognition Teaching Objective	Language Comprehension Teaching Objective
What's It Made Of?	• Strand 5: Recognise and use alternative ways of pronouncing the graphemes already taught, for example, that the graphemes 'wr' are pronounced 'r' and the graphemes 'kn' are pronounced 'n'.	• Strand 8: Distinguish fiction and non-fiction texts and the different purposes for reading them.
I Take Care of My Dog	• Strand 5: Read more challenging texts which can be decoded using their acquired phonic knowledge and skills, along with automatic recognition of high frequency words.	• Strand 7: Make predictions showing an understanding of ideas, events and characters.
Where Is Joe?	• Strand 5: Apply phonic knowledge and skills as the prime approach to reading and spelling unfamiliar words that are not completely decodable.	• Strand 7: Recognise the main elements that shape different texts.
Make Your Own Monster!	• Strand 5: Identify the constituent parts of two-syllable and three-syllable words to support the application of phonic knowledge and skills.	• Strand 7: Recognise the main elements that shape different texts (instructional texts).

• You will find full teaching notes in the Teaching Version for each book.

• For a chart showing you the strand objectives of the renewed Framework, please see page 185 of this guide.

Genre	Common Words	Linked Rigby Star Independent Reader	
Report	here • made • many • more some • these • what		Thematic link: Materials
Recount	after • be • his • much some • take • then very • water • when with		Thematic link: Likes and dislikes
Signs, labels, captions	are • by • do • first •from has • next • of • over saw • that • them then • these • took very • which	No linked title	
Instructions	could • first • how • make now • them • then • this two • what • your	No linked title	

Green Level: Fiction

Title	Word Recognition Teaching Objective	Language Comprehension Teaching Objective
The Singing Giant (story)	• Strand 5: Recognise and use alternative ways of pronouncing the graphemes already taught, for example, that the grapheme 'g' is pronounced differently in 'George' and 'garden'.	• Strand 7: Identify the main events and characters in stories.
The Singing Giant (play)	• Strand 5: Read more challenging texts which can be decoded using their acquired phonic knowledge and skills, along with automatic recognition of high frequency words.	• Strand 4: Act out their own and well-known stories, using voices for characters.
Clever Chick	• Strand 5: Identify the constituent parts of two-syllable and three-syllable words to support the application of phonic knowledge and skills.	• Strand 8: Visualise and comment on events, characters and ideas, making imaginative links to own experiences.
Josie Goes on Holiday	• Strand 5: Recognise automatically an increasing number of familiar high frequency words.	• Strand 7: Identify the main events and characters in stories.

• You will find full teaching notes in the Teaching Version for each book.

• For a chart showing you the strand objectives of the renewed Framework, please see page 185 of this guide.

Genre	Common Words	Linked Rigby Star Independent Reader	
A tale with a traditional character, but modern setting and language.	must • night • over • people would(n't)		Thematic link: Traditional story characters
A play version of a story featuring a traditional character.	again • door • house • much must • next • night • not now • that		Skills focus: To read with expression
A modern story, with a predictable structure, based on a traditional theme.	as • jump(ed) • much ran • than • very		Skills focus: Characters
A modern realistic story with a camping holiday setting.	could(n't) • good • got • so time • took • us • very		Skills focus: Identifying main events

Green Level: Fiction (continued)

Title	Word Recognition Teaching Objective	Language Comprehension Teaching Objective
Yo-Yo a Go-Go	• Strand 5: Read more challenging texts which can be decoded using their acquired phonic knowledge and skills, along with automatic recognition of high frequency words.	• Strand 7: Identify the main events and characters in stories.
Stone Soup	• Strand 5: Read more challenging texts which can be decoded using their acquired phonic knowledge and skills, along with automatic recognition of high frequency words.	• Strand 7: Recognise the main elements that shape different texts.
The Wind and the Sun	• Strand 5: Apply phonic knowledge and skills as the prime approach to reading and spelling unfamiliar words that are not completely decodable.	• Strand 7: Use syntax and context when reading for meaning.
The Fantastic Pumpkin	• Strand 5: Read phonically decodable two-syllable and three-syllable words.	• Strand 7: Make predictions showing an understanding of ideas, events and characters.

• You will find full teaching notes in the Teaching Version for each book.

• For a chart showing you the strand objectives of the renewed Framework, please see page 185 of this guide

Genre	Common Words	Linked Rigby Star Independent Reader	
A modern realistic story with a familiar setting and predictable structure.	again • our • put • school were		Thematic link: Toys and games
A traditional tale with the theme of trickery.	again • from • had • here make • man • put • people some • would		Thematic link: Traditional tale
An Aesop Fable.	down • first • man • off than • that • there		Thematic link: Fable / fairy story
A fantasy story with a familiar setting and predictable structure.	as • from • just • man more • people • some		Thematic link: Amazing vegetables!

Green Level: Phonics

Title	Word Recognition Teaching Objective	Focused Phonic Opportunities
Josie and the Puppy	• Strand 5: Read and spell phonically decodable two-syllable and three-syllable words.	• Decoding words with different spellings of the 'or' phoneme • Decoding words with more than one syllable
Elvis and the Space Junk	• Strand 5: Recognise and use alternative ways of spelling the phonemes already taught.	• Decoding words with different spellings of the 'air' and 'ear' phonemes
Big Spider	• Strand 5: Identify the constituent parts of two-syllable and three-syllable words to support the application of phonic knowledge and skills.	• Decoding words with more than one syllable
Too Much Talk!	• Strand 5: Read and spell phonically decodable two-syllable and three-syllable words.	• Decoding words with different spellings of the 'ee' phoneme • Decoding words with more than one syllable

• You will find full teaching notes in the Teaching Version for each book.

• For a chart showing you the strand objectives of the renewed Framework, please see page 185 of this guide.

Language Comprehension Teaching Objective	Common Words	Genre
• Strand 8: Visualise and comment on events, characters and ideas, making imaginative links to their own experiences.	so • she • went • with • mum dog • to • the • him • how after • back • then • took laugh(ed) • little • like • they home • called • an • old made • bed • said • had • put	Modern realistic story
• Strand 7: Identify the main events and characters in stories.	was • in • a • there • went • out of • very • got • could • see down • where • am • I • said just • then • came • look • saw some • not • my • all • next jump(ed) • what	Story with patterned structure
• Strand 7: Make predictions showing an understanding of ideas, events and characters.	once • there • by • have • is be • like • that • would • tree more • then • his • came what • then • come • how • all	Rhyming text
• Strand 7: Identify the main events and characters in stories.	one • his • pull(ed) • out did • not • now • who • that not • so • down • then • time how • yes • after • can't	Fantasy story

Green Level: Non-fiction

Title	Word Recognition Teaching Objective	Language Comprehension Teaching Objective
Animal Feet	• Strand 5: Identify the constituent parts of two-syllable words to support the application of phonic knowledge and skills.	• Strand 8: Distinguish fiction and non-fiction texts and the different purposes for reading them.
How to make a Bird Feeder	• Strand 5: Read and spell phonically decodable two-syllable words.	• Strand 7: Explore the effect of patterns of language and repeated words and phrases.
Camping	• Strand 5: Read more challenging texts which can be decoded using their acquired phonic knowledge and skills, along with automatic recognition of high frequency words.	• Strand 7: Find specific information in simple texts.
How Does Water Change?	• Strand 5: Recognise and use alternative ways of spelling the phonemes already taught, for example that the /e/ sound can be spelt with 'ea' and 'e'.	• Strand 7: Find specific information in simple texts.

• You will find full teaching notes in the Teaching Version for each book.

• For a chart showing you the strand objectives of the renewed Framework, please see page 185 of this guide.

Genre	Common Words	Linked Rigby Star Independent Reader	
Report	an • down • from tree • water • with		Thematic link: Animal body parts
Instructions	about • from • make many • now • one put • tree • will • your		Thematic link: Instructional language
Recount	did • how • in • our • them those • two • we • what with • us • you	No linked title	
Explanation	an • as • be • from • is • it of • on • water • when where • you	No linked title	

Assessment and Rigby Star Guided Reading

Assessment and guided reading

Guided reading works well when the children in a group are working at approximately the same level. There should be a teaching/learning objective for each guided reading session which is appropriate for all children in the group and is at the cutting edge of each child's learning. Careful assessment enables you to place the children on an appropriate level of Rigby Star and in ability groups.

Assessment in Rigby Star

In Year One it is useful to monitor children's developing reading behaviours, including their common (high frequency) word and phonic knowledge.

The development of reading behaviours through Rigby Star levels closely follows those described in *Book Bands for Guided Reading*. Rigby Star provides progressive opportunities for phonic teaching and opportunities for introducing the most common (high frequency) words.

Rigby Star provides a range of assessment materials for use in Year One. The materials support summative assessment at regular points to check children's progress and amend the groupings if necessary. There is also support for the ongoing assessment that is integral to every guided reading lesson.
- Reading Behaviour Checklists
- Phonics Checklists
- Common Word Checklist
- Children's reading and writing target sheets
- Self-Assessment Sheets for each colour level

Assessment for Learning

Assessment for Learning describes assessment activities that give evidence of where learners are in their learning and helps to inform decisions about the next steps to take.

Children's learning improves when assessment is used to inform teaching. They are more confident and motivated when they are actively involved in their own learning. Children need to be given effective feedback so that they can understand what they need to do to make further progress.

Guided reading lessons provide an ideal context in which to apply the principles of Assessment for Learning. Each lesson is carefully planned and has a clear focus for learning.

The teacher starts by sharing the learning objectives with the children. During and after reading the teacher observes carefully and uses prompts and questions to ensure that children know what they need to do to achieve the learning objectives. The final part of each session involves feedback related to the learning objectives. Children's successes are identified and they consider what they need to work on next. The teacher can then complete the Group Reading Record (see page 58 of this guide) to record this assessment.

Applying the principles of Assessment for Learning within Rigby Star Guided Reading

Conditions for learning

Children need to learn *how* to learn. In the context of reading, children need to have an understanding of what they need to do to improve as readers. They need a framework and language for talking about which skills work and identifying what they need to work on next. The Self-Assessment Sheets for the Yellow, Blue and Green levels provide a framework for this. The sheets can be discussed in whole class sessions and reading behaviours can be demonstrated in shared reading so that the children understand the statements.

Planning

The teaching objectives in the Rigby Star Teaching Versions provide a clear focus for the learning in each lesson. These need to be introduced in a way that the children can understand and can be referred to during the lesson. Teachers can summarise the key points that will help children to achieve the objective/s – these are presented as success criteria. The success criteria help to focus children's learning and provide a framework for discussion and feedback at the end of the lesson.

Day-to-day assessment

When children are reading independently in the guided reading lesson, the teacher is able to focus on how learning is progressing. He or she can observe, ask questions, analyse and discuss the books to check children's understanding, correct misconceptions and praise successful skills and behaviours. The Teaching Versions provide detailed support for this in the Observe and Prompt sections. The photocopy masters have independent follow-up activities that help teachers check children's understanding.

Feedback on learning

The final part of each guided reading lesson provides an opportunity for oral feedback to children. The teacher talks about successful reading skills and refers back to the success criteria so that children can reflect on their own learning. Teachers can talk positively about any difficulties that were encountered to help children feel that they can learn from their mistakes and build on them to improve as readers.

Assessing reading behaviours

Working with a group of children on a regular basis gives you opportunities to assess each child's strengths, knowledge and application of skills. These close observations enable you to check that the child is learning how to read new texts independently, and to make accurate judgements about the next learning goals or objectives for each child.

The Rigby Star Teaching Versions highlight opportunities for assessing children's reading behaviours during a guided reading lesson. They also include specific assessment questions to help you assess each child's level of understanding of the teaching objectives for the lesson. By using open-ended questions you can encourage children to think about the skills they have used and check their understanding, for example, 'What did you do to solve that new word…?', 'Why do you think that the character behaved like that…?', 'Where is there another example of…?'

Valuable information may be obtained from informal observations of this kind and can be recorded on the child's Reading Behaviour Checklist to provide an on-going record of the child's progress. These checklists are provided on pages 55–57. Children can be given oral feedback on their learning at the end of the guided reading lesson. You can use the Self-Assessment Sheets to get the children involved in identifying what they can do as readers and thinking about their next steps.

Children working at Rigby Star Yellow, Blue and Green levels will have the following reading behaviours.

Yellow level

Children reading Yellow level are cross-checking all sources of information more quickly as they read. They search for information in print and use phonic knowledge to predict, confirm or attempt new words while reading. They are also reading more naturally and expressively, taking note of punctuation, grammar and oral language rhythms as they read.

Blue level

Children reading Blue level are managing a greater variety of texts and re-read to clarify precise meaning. They are reading with phrasing and self-correct more rapidly.

Green level

Children reading Green level are reading fluently, paying attention to punctuation. They can read a variety of texts effectively with fuller understanding of character and plot. They can discuss information in a text, and talk about text features.

Reading Behaviour Checklists

Each level of Rigby Star is accompanied by a Reading Behaviour Checklist. Record the child's level of achievement on the Reading Behaviour Checklist by using a simple coding system.

Tick and date the '0' box

If a child does not seem to be using or displaying the skill (e.g. child reads unnaturally with little consideration of oral language rhythms, punctuation or grammar).

Tick and date the '1' box

If a child seems to partially understand or use the skill, or if there is some evidence that the child has the skill (e.g. the child reads naturally but does not always respond to punctuation).

Tick and date the '2' box

If the child is able to understand and use the skill (e.g. the child reads naturally, paying attention to punctuation and grammar and re-reads to enhance phrasing and clarify precise meaning).

Reading Behaviour Checklists for Yellow, Blue and Green levels are to be found on pages 55–57 of this guide.

Assessing word recognition knowledge

In Year One children are using their phonic knowledge and skills as the prime approach to reading. They are also using their knowledge of common words, and will recognise a greater number of these common words automatically.

Phonics checklist

Rigby Star Guided Reading books provide opportunities for children to put into practice the phonics they will be learning in the whole class teaching of phonics.

Two Phonics Checklists are provided on pages 64 and 65 of this guide:

- *Blending phonemes; one-, two- and three-syllable words*
  This checklist begins with one-syllable words, containing adjacent consonants, to enable you to check that the children have mastered sounding and blending phonemes all through the word, from left to right, by the start of Year One. Then two- and three-syllable words are provided for you to check that children can identify where to break a multi-syllabic word, in order to tackle the whole word using their phonic skills.

- *Vowel digraphs*
  This checklist enables you to check children's understanding of vowel digraphs. You can use this checklist for Yellow, Blue and Green levels, depending on your particular group.

Common word checklist

The books in Rigby Star have been structured with a progression in common (high frequency) words. It is useful to assess children's ability to recognise each common word in the context of a sentence, in isolation, and to write it. A Common Word Checklist is provided on page 66 of this guide.

Children's self-assessment

Children's assessment of their own progress encourages them to take responsibility for their learning. They can help to set their own reading and writing targets.

Illustrated targets

Illustrated targets for children's reading and writing in Year One are provided on pages 59 and 60 of this guide. These can be used as a record of achievement which can be stored and sent home so that parents and carers can share in their child's progress.

Self-Assessment Sheets

Children can be involved in assessing their own progress as readers and deciding what they need to work on next. The Self-Assessment Sheets are designed to support this process by:
- identifying the key reading skills at each reading level in language that children can understand
- giving children the chance to identify what they can do
- helping children think about other skills that they need to work on.

The Self-Assessment Sheets are based on the Reading Behaviour Checklist for each level.

How to use the Self-Assessment Sheets in guided reading lessons

Copy a Self-Assessment Sheet for each child in the guided reading group. You may wish to laminate them so that children can re-use them in several guided reading lessons.

The skills and behaviours are characteristic of readers at a particular level and the children will be using an increasing number of them as they read the texts in successive sessions. Initially the statements may need some explanation. You could demonstrate what particular statements mean as part of shared reading sessions for the whole year-group. For example, to explain 'I repeated a sentence to make the meaning clearer' (Blue level), demonstrate how to solve new words using decoding skills before going back to the start of the sentence and reading more quickly to gain more understanding.

Before a guided reading lesson

After the Walkthrough/Tuning In you can focus on one or two statements from the sheet to use as a skills check. Explain how these skills will be particularly useful when reading this text and will help with the learning objectives. You may wish to remind individual children about particular skills that they are working on.

During a guided reading lesson

Prompt children if necessary so that they understand how these skills will help them become more confident and fluent. Praise children as you see them using a particular skill so that they recognise when they have done it, for example, 'I like the way you sounded out that word...'.

After a guided reading lesson

Use the Self-Assessment Sheets as part of the Revisit and Respond time. Ask children to think about successful skills they used to solve new words or to correct mistakes, and remind them of things that you saw. Give a little time for each child to identify which skills they used. Talk about ways that they could use these again, for example, 'You corrected a mistake by yourself. I expect you will be able to check that your reading makes sense the next time you read a book.' Children could go on to think about the skills that they did not use this time. Talk about which ones they use most and which ones they need to work on.

Writing

Useful information can be obtained from children's writing. There is a photocopiable writing activity to accompany each book in Rigby Star. These may be used to assess children's word recognition.

Managing progression in guided reading

How do I match the child to a Rigby Star level?

Use your knowledge of the children and information from the child's Reading Behaviour Checklist at Foundation Stage to decide initially where to place children on Rigby Star levels. There may be some children coming into Year One who are not yet ready to read Yellow level. Information on these children's Reading Behaviour Checklists from Foundation Stage will help you place them on the Red level.

When do I re-group children?

In guided reading it seems to work well to carry out half-termly assessment and to re-group the children if necessary. In the last week before half term, assessments can be carried out either during a guided reading session or as a separate assessment outside the reading session. Use one of the books from the Rigby Star level the child is reading. Use the assessment points in the Teaching Version to help you assess the child's grasp of the teaching objectives of that book. Use this in combination with information from the child's Reading Behaviour Checklist and the Phonics and Common Word Checklists, to decide if the child is reading at the right level. If the child needs extra practice at the same level you can use *Book Bands for Guided Reading* to match books from other programmes to Rigby Star.

If a child is making quick progress, i.e. reading each new text quickly and making few if any mistakes, this lack of challenge may alert you to move the child up a level. Using information on the child's Reading Behaviour Checklist and your own knowledge of the child will help you place him or her on the appropriate level of Rigby Star.

If a child is struggling in his or her current ability group, you can use the same assessment procedure to move the child to a more appropriate level of Rigby Star.

A photocopiable Group Reading Record is provided on page 58. This enables you to track the progress of individual children and groups during the guided reading session.

Identifying progression in non-fiction reading

Children may react to non-fiction texts in a different way to their handling of fiction. Key features of successful non-fiction reading include: cross-checking all sources of information more quickly, beginning to notice differences in fiction and non-fiction, and recognising different ways of presenting information.

Reading Behaviour Checklist

Yellow Level

NAME

READING BEHAVIOUR	SCORE		
	0	1	2
Follows print with eyes only.			
Finger-points only at points of difficulty.			
Reads naturally, taking note of punctuation, grammar and oral language rhythms.			
Cross-checks all sources of information more quickly when reading.			
Analyses print to predict, confirm or attempt new words while reading.			
Notices relationships between one text and another.			
Uses decoding skills to tackle new and more complex words.			
Predicts content in more detail.			
Reads and uses simple captions, charts and instructions. (NF)			
Recognises layout of different types of text. (NF)			

Assessment record

The following scores indicate level of each child's reading behaviours.

0 = child has no understanding   1 = child has partial understanding   2 = child has full understanding

Tick and date each entry to track child's progress.

NF means non-fiction.

Reading Behaviour Checklist

Blue Level

NAME

READING BEHAVIOUR	SCORE		
	0	1	2
Self-corrects more rapidly on the run.			
Re-reads to enhance phrasing and clarify precise meaning.			
Solves new words using decoding skills along with attention to meaning.			
Discusses content of a text in a manner which indicates precise understanding.			
Manages a greater range of text types and genres, and adjusts reading accordingly.			

Assessment record

The following scores indicate level of each child's reading behaviours.

0 = child has no understanding   1 = child has partial understanding   2 = child has full understanding

Tick and date each entry to track child's progress.

Reading Behaviour Checklist

Green Level

NAME

READING BEHAVIOUR	SCORE		
	0	1	2
Reads fluently with attention to punctuation.			
Solves new words using decoding skills while attending to meaning and syntax.			
Tracks visually additional lines of print without difficulty.			
Manages effectively a growing variety of texts, and adjusts reading accordingly.			
Discusses, interprets and talks about information contained in the text, for example, features of the text, character, plot.			

Assessment record

The following scores indicate level of each child's reading behaviours.

0 = child has no understanding   1 = child has partial understanding   2 = child has full understanding

Tick and date each entry to track child's progress.

© Harcourt Education Ltd, 2007

Group Reading Record

NAMES OF CHILDREN

TITLE OF BOOK

MAIN TEACHING OBJECTIVES

TEACHING OBJECTIVES ACHIEVED

BEHAVIOUR OBSERVED

INDIVIDUAL TARGETS

My Reading Targets

NAME	TEACHER
	TERM
COMMENT	CARER'S SIGNATURE

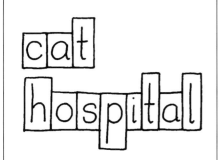

I can recognise different shaped words.

I know how to blend phonemes.

. B

I can recognise full stops and capital letters.

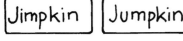
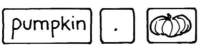

I can put the words of a sentence in order.

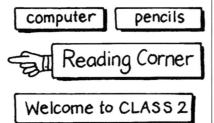

I can read captions, signs and labels.

I know the difference between fiction and non-fiction books.

I can concentrate enough to read the whole book.

I can discuss the characters.

I can talk about the story setting.

My Writing Targets

NAME	TEACHER
	TERM
COMMENT	CARER'S SIGNATURE

I can spell words which are new to me.

I can spell new words using phonics.

I can make my own word bank.

I can plan, write and make my own book.

I can write about my own experiences.

I can write sentences about a character from a story.

I can write my own poem.

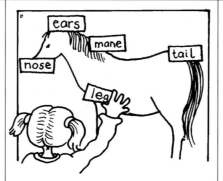

I can write my own lists.

I know how to write instructions and rules.

My Self-Assessment Sheet

Name ....

Which lily pads will the frog hop on today?

I sounded out some words using phonics.

I read some words I knew already.

I used the punctuation.

I checked that a sentence made sense.

I checked that a word looked right and sounded right.

I only pointed at the words I was stuck on.

I corrected a mistake by myself.

I made my reading sound like talking.

My Self-Assessment Sheet

Name ....

Which puddles will the duck paddle in today?

I solved a new word using phonics and then checked that it made sense.

I repeated a sentence to make the meaning clearer.

I used speech marks to help me add expression.

I knew what to do if I got stuck: I looked carefully at the word and sounded it out from left to right.

I corrected my own mistakes while I was reading.

I talked about what I had read.

My Self-Assessment Sheet

Name ....

Which leaves will the caterpillar nibble today?

I solved new words using phonics and checked that they made sense in the sentence.

I read at a good speed and I noticed the punctuation.

I corrected a mistake by myself and repeated the sentence to check the meaning.

I read a page with lots of lines of print.

STORIES: I knew what to expect in this type of story.

INFORMATION: I knew how to use the features of this book.

STORIES: I noticed speech marks and used expression for speech.

INFORMATION: I talked about the information I found out from this book.

STORIES: I talked about the story and the characters.

Phonics Checklist

Yellow, Blue and Green Levels

NAME

One-syllable words	Can blend orally	Can segment orally
lamp		
sleep		
wish		
flip		
brick		
shark		
plant		
stand		
string		
drink		

Two- and three-syllable words	Can read the word	Can syllabify the word
monster		
shopping		
dolphin		
away		
dinner		
yesterday		
shimmering		
holiday		
tomorrow		
animals		

Instructions

When reading longer words, children need to be able to split the words into syllables. Children should be taught that every syllable has a vowel in it.

Use the two- and three-syllable words to check children's understanding of this rule.

Tick and date each entry to track child's progress.

Yellow, Blue and Green Levels

NAME

Vowel digraphs	Can read the word	Can segment the phonemes	Can blend the phonemes	Can write the word
pay				
plate				
brain				
free				
tea				
seen				
fly				
line				
bright				
toe				
slow				
gold				
blue				
stool				
cute				
hard				
toy				
join				
down				
loud				
house				
stood				
should				
book				
fall				
stork				
dawn				
herb				
girl				
nurse				
care				
fair				

Instructions

Tick and date each entry to track child's progess.

Common Word Checklist

Yellow, Blue and Green Levels

NAME

Common word	1	2	3	Common word	1	2	3
about				make			
asked				man			
away				Mr			
by				Mrs			
called				oh			
came				old			
children				one			
come				out			
could				over			
day				people			
did				said			
do				saw			
don't				so			
from				some			
good				their			
have				then			
help				there			
here				time			
house				very			
how				want			
I'm				water			
it's				went			
just				were			
like				what			
little				when			
looked				with			
made				your			

Instructions

Use this chart to record how well the child can both read and write common words in Yellow, Blue and Green Levels.

1 = can recognise the word in context   2 = can recognise the word in isolation

3 = can write the word without copying.

Tick and date each entry to track child's progress.

Name

Put the sentences in the right order.

Josie had a book.

Josie said, "Go away, baby!"

The baby wanted to play.

Josie said, "Yes, baby. Look!"

Josie had a farm.

The baby wanted to look.

Josie and the Baby
Skill: sequencing

RIGBY
star ★

Name

WRITING ★ FICTION

1.2

YELLOW LEVEL

Write what Josie says to the baby.

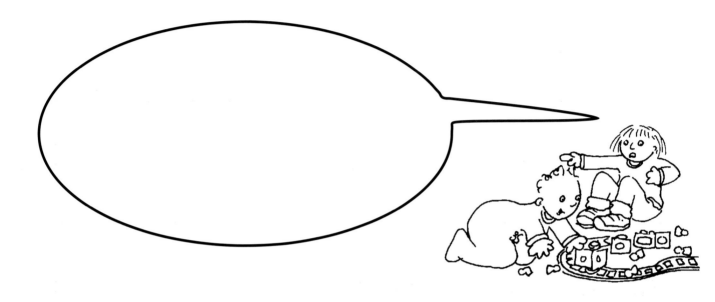

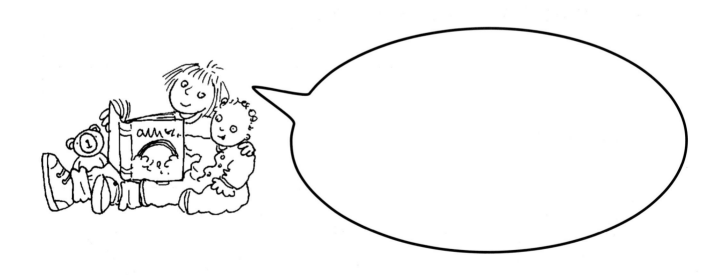

Josie and the Baby

Skill: writing dialogue in speech bubbles

RIGBY
star

© Harcourt Education Ltd, 2007

Match the character to the words.

Look out! Look out!		
I like my little balloons!		
All my balloons went pop!		
You can have my balloon.		
I like my blue balloon!		

RIGBY
star ★

Write what Hedgehog says to Kangaroo.

Add the missing words.
Put in the correct order.

 Joe put his coat _____.

 "Can you help me get _____?"

 He put his bear _____.

 "Can you help me get _____?"

 "Can you help me get _____?"

| up | down | in | on | down |

Grandpa

Skill: using key words in context

RIGBY
star ★

© Harcourt Education Ltd, 2007

Name

Write what happens next.

Grandpa and Joe went to the fair.

" _____?" said Joe.

" _____?" said Grandpa.

Grandpa

Skill: high frequency words in sentence construction

RIGBY
star

Name ....

Match the days to the sentences.

On Monday	Dad gave her a book.	
On Tuesday	Aunt Ann went into hospital.	
On Wednesday	We gave her some flowers.	
On Thursday	She came home with us.	
On Friday	Mum gave her a plant.	
On Saturday	Grandpa gave her some fruit.	
On Sunday	Gran gave her some sweets.	

What a Week!

Skill: sequencing days of the week

RIGBY **star** ★

© Harcourt Education Ltd, 2007

Name ....

WRITING ★ FICTION

4.2

YELLOW LEVEL

Fill in the missing words on the calendar.

_____	_____	_____
15 May	16 May	17 May

_____	_____	_____
18 May	19 May	20 May

_____
21 May

What a Week!

Skill: writing – days of the week

RIGBY
star

© Harcourt Education Ltd, 2007

Name

Stick the words on the map to show where the family went.

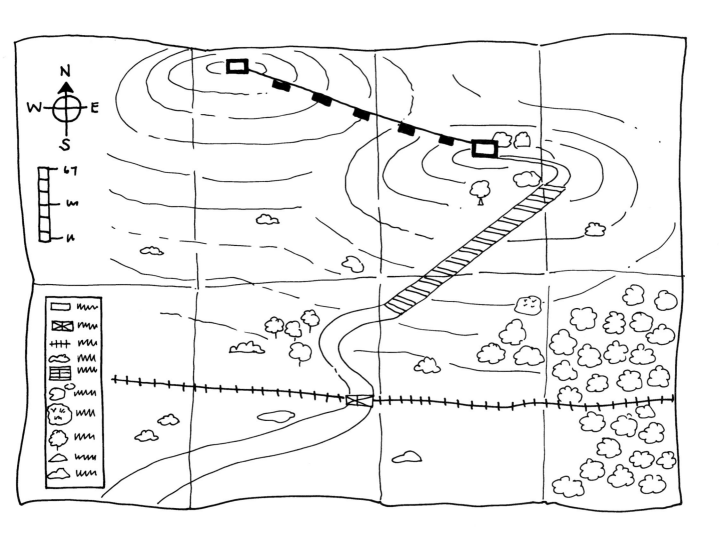

| up in the lift | up the steps |
| up the path | up the road |

Name

....

Write what happens next.

We went up the road.

_____ _____

_____ _____ _____

_____ _____ _____

_____ _____ _____

_____ _____ _____ _____

Put the sentences in the right order.

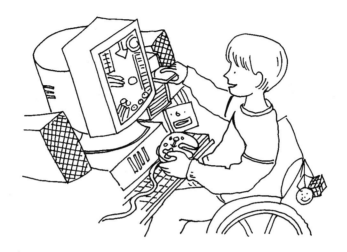

Pete helped Mum to make the sandwiches.

"Grandma's here!" said Dad.

Pete had a new computer game.

Pete and Grandma played all day.

Pete helped Dad to make the bed.

The Computer Game

Skill: sequencing

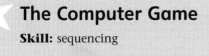

RIGBY
star ★

© Harcourt Education Ltd, 2007

WRITING ★ FICTION

6.2

YELLOW LEVEL

Use speech bubbles to retell the story.

Match the character to the words they say.

"Is he under here?"	
"He is not under here."	
"Where did he go?"	
"Is he up here?"	
"He is not down here."	
"He is not in here."	

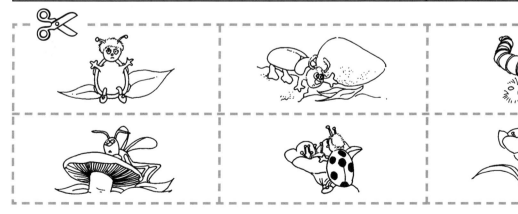

Write in the missing words.

Is he _____ here?

He is ____ under _____ .

Is ___ ___ here?

He ___ not ___ _____ .

He ___ ___ _____ here.

Put the sentences in the right order.

"Have you got everything?" asked Dad.

Knock! Knock!

"Yes," said Colin.

"I forgot my coat!"

"Yes, I have," said Colin.

"Goodbye!"

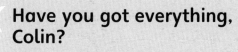

Put the right words in the speech bubbles.

Match the characters to what they eat.

I like to eat corn.	
I like to eat hay.	
I like to eat grass.	
I like to eat bread.	
I like to eat animals.	

Name

....

WRITING ★ FICTION

9.2

YELLOW LEVEL

Write in the missing words.

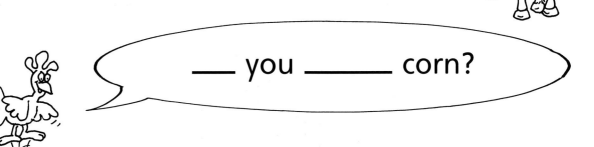

What ___ you _____ to eat?

Do ___ _____ hay?

___ you _____ corn?

__ __ _____ bread?

What __ _____ __ _____ __ ____?

The Lion's Dinner – A Play

Skill: completing dialogue with high frequency words

RIGBY
star

© Harcourt Education Ltd, 2007

Name

Put these sentences in the right order.

"Can you look at my teeth?" I asked.

The dentist looked at my dinosaur's teeth.

"You can have a **big** sticker!"

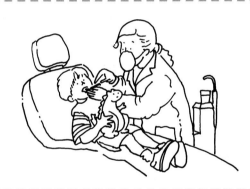

"Can I have a little sticker?" I asked.

One day, I went to the dentist.

The dentist looked at my teeth.

Name

Write the right words in the speech bubbles.

Write **s**, **sh** or **sp** under each picture.

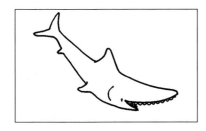      

___sh___   _____   _____

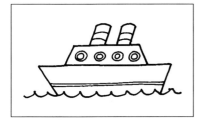      

_____   _____   _____

      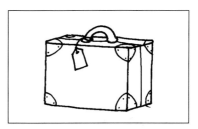

_____   _____   _____

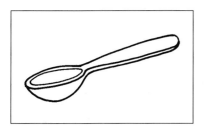   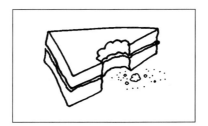   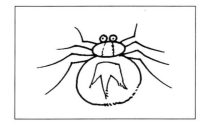

_____   _____   _____

Super Shopping

Skill: identifying initial phonemes s, sh, sp

RIGBY
star

Name

....

Write in the missing words.

The _____ shop sold _____ .

The _____ shop sold _____ .

The _____ shop sold _____ .

The _____ shop sold _____ .

The _____ shop sold _____ .

The _____ shop sold _____ .

RIGBY
star

Name

Read each sentence then circle **Yes** or **No**.

Mum got some shoes.	**Yes**	**No**
I got a helmet.	**Yes**	**No**
My brother got a book.	**Yes**	**No**
Mum got a car.	**Yes**	**No**
Mum got a book.	**Yes**	**No**
My brother got a helmet.	**Yes**	**No**
I got a book.	**Yes**	**No**
We went to the shoe shop.	**Yes**	**No**

Where's Our Car?

Skill: comprehension

RIGBY
star

© Harcourt Education Ltd, 2007

Name

Write in the signs.

page 3

page 5

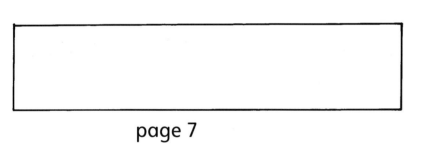

page 7

page 11

page 9

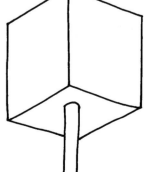

page 15

Where's Our Car?

Skill: identifying and writing signs

WRITING ★ FICTION

12.2

YELLOW LEVEL

Cross out the wrong words.

Chelsea said, "Don't push pull."
Harry pushed pulled.
The door opened.

Chelsea said, "Don't push pull."
Harry pushed pulled.
The door opened.

Harry didn't pull push.
Harry didn't pull push.
The door did didn't open!

Name

Write in the missing words in the pictures and the sentences.

push + ed = _____

pull + ed = _____

Harry _____

Harry _____

Harry didn't _____

He didn't _____

Name

Put each picture in the right box.

cr	sn	gr	sp

Name

Write what the spider says.

Put the two parts of each sentence together.

The keys are	on the table.
The books are	on the chair.
The sandwiches are	in the cupboard.
The bags are	in your pocket.
The gloves are	on your head.
The glasses are	in the drawer.
The pens are	in the fridge.

Rush Hour

Skill: matching words to make sentences

Write questions in the speech bubbles.
Use the words below.

| keys | my | are | books |
| Where | pens | sandwiches | |

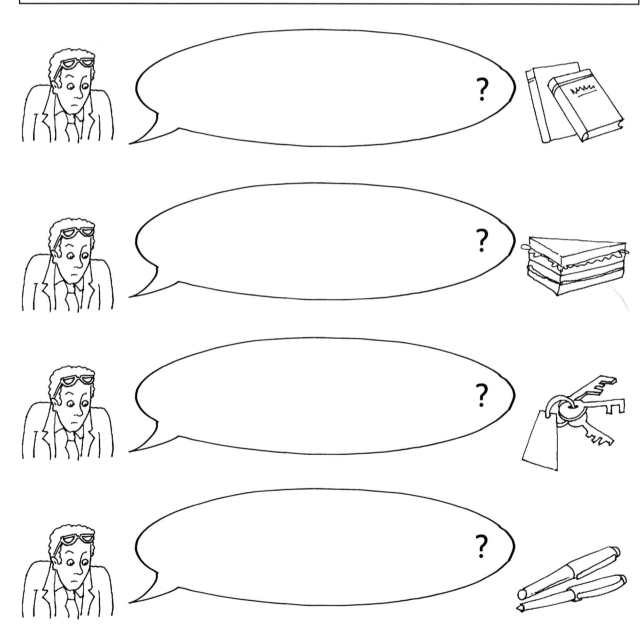

Put the sentences in the right order.

"I like this popcorn," he said.

Jack and his dad went to the cinema.

"I like this drink," he said.

Jack got up. He wanted to go to the toilet.

"Come on, Dad," said Jack, but Dad was asleep.

Then Jack saw a friend.

Be Quiet!

Skill: sequencing

RIGBY
star★

Name

Write what Jack says.

Name

Sequence the sentences.

Josie and Dad rubbed the car.

Dad got a tin of wax.

Josie got all the junk out of the back of the car.

They put the wax on the car.

They got all the mud off the car.

Josie put the wax on a rag.

Name

....

Write instructions for
cleaning a car.

What you need

_____   _____

_____   _____

_____   _____

What you do

_____

_____

_____

_____

_____

_____

_____

_____

_____

Name

Sequence the story.

On Monday	I play ping-pong with a bat.
On Tuesday	I play chess with a king.
On Wednesday	I play tag with my dog.
On Thursday	I play IT with my pet.
On Friday	I play up with my dad.
On Saturday	I play snap with a crab.
On Sunday	I play dot-to-dot with a pen.

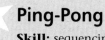

Ping-Pong

Skill: sequencing days of the week

Name

....

Write the boy's diary for one of the days in the story.

Diary

On
_____

_____

I
_____

_____

_____

_____

_____

Name

Sequence the story.

Name

WRITING ★ PHONICS
3.2
YELLOW LEVEL

Fill in the missing words.

| Josh | Jill | bent | next |
| and | said | she | |

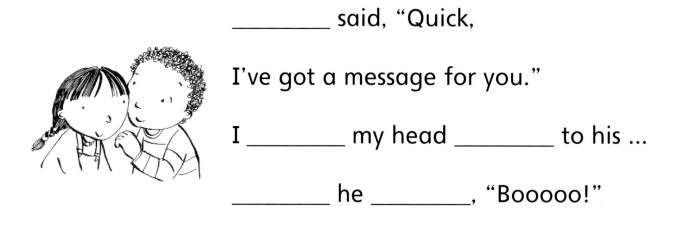

_____ said, "Quick,

I've got a message for you."

I _____ my head _____ to his ...

_____ he _____, "Booooo!"

_____ said, "Look,

I have something to tell you."

I _____ my head _____ to hers ...

and _____ said, "Boooooo!"

★★★ **Booooo!**
Skill: writing CVCC words

RIGBY
star ★

© Harcourt Education Ltd, 2007

Put the sentences in the right order.

This is the boat that Bert built.

It bobs on the waves.

This is the bird Bert quickly saves.

And this is the gold that Bert unlocks.

Bert and the bird, afloat on their boat.

This is a cliff with deep, dark caves.

This is Bert's boat.

This is a box that sits on the rocks.

This is the key that opens the box.

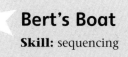

Bert's Boat

Skill: sequencing

Write a list of things Bert will buy with the gold.

_____

_____

_____

_____

_____

_____

★★★ **Bert's Boat**

Skill: writing a list

RIGBY
star ★

Name

Read each sentence then circle **Yes** or **No**.

The girls said, "You are too little."	Yes	No
The boys said, "You are too big."	Yes	No
Sam did not have a ball.	Yes	No
A ball came over the wall.	Yes	No
It was Sam's ball.	Yes	No
The girl said she had lost her ball.	Yes	No
Sam played with Sam.	Yes	No

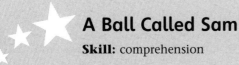

A Ball Called Sam

Skill: comprehension

Name ....

Write your own ending.
What does Sam say to Sam?

Name

....

Match the sentences to the pictures.

| The cat said, "You are ugly. Go away and don't come back." | "I don't like being the grey duckling," said Josie. |
| "Wow! The grey duckling has become a beautiful swan!" said the white swans. | "Josie, you can be the grey duckling," said Mrs Sanchez. |

Rewrite the story as a play.

yellow duckling: _____

_____

cat: _____

_____

dog: _____

_____

white swans: _____

_____

Josie and the Play

Skill: rewriting as play

RIGBY
star ★

© Harcourt Education Ltd, 2007

Name

···

Find and colour the rhyming words.
Use a different colour for each rhyme.

There is a terrible tiger under my bed.

I can see his tail.

I can see his head.

"Terrible Tiger, go away!

Terrible Tiger, please don't stay!"

I can see his teeth in his terrible jaws.

I can see his feet with their terrible claws.

"Terrible Tiger, go away!

Terrible Tiger, please don't stay!"

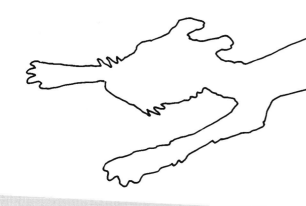

★★★ **Terrible Tiger**

Skill: identifying rhyme

WRITING ★ FICTION

3.2

BLUE LEVEL

Choose a part of the story.
Write what the boy says.

★★★ **Terrible Tiger**

Skill: recalling and writing a sentence

RIGBY
star

Name

Fill in the space log to show who said what on each planet.

	Blue Planet	Red Planet	Purple Planet
(ant)			(purple planet)
(dog)		(red planet)	
(bird/elephant)	(blue planet)		

✂

Yesss. I don't like it here.	It's too hot. I don't like it here.	This planet is just right.
I love it!	This blue planet is freezing cold!	Phew! This red planet is boiling hot!

Name

....

Make two of your own creatures.

elephant   +   bird   =   elebird

_____

cat   lion   shark

dinosaur   butterfly   ladybird

_____ + _____ = _____

_____ + _____ = _____

RIGBY
star

Name

What did they say?
Match the words to the characters.

He has my bat!	We can't play now!
He has my new hat!	He took my bat.
He took my ball.	Don't be sad. I've got an idea.
What did Bully Bear do?	He took my new hat.

Bully Bear

Skill: matching words to characters

Rewrite these parts of the story as a play.
The first part has been done for you.

Moose: What did Bully Bear do?

Little Bear: _____

Raccoon: _____

Squirrel: _____

Moose: _____

_____

Bully Bear: _____

_____

Moose: _____

Bully Bear: _____

Name

Read each sentence then circle **Yes** or **No**.

Josie and Mum went out.	**Yes** **No**
Mum went to get a new coat	**Yes** **No**
The fluffy coat was too little.	**Yes** **No**
The red coat was too little.	**Yes** **No**
The new coat was green.	**Yes** **No**
Dad said, "Do you like it?"	**Yes** **No**
Josie went to school in a red coat.	**Yes** **No**
Josie said, "I've got a new coat!"	**Yes** **No**

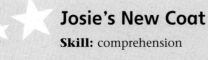

Josie's New Coat

Skill: comprehension

Retell the story.

Josie and Mum went out. They went to . . .

Josie wanted a fluffy coat but . . .

Mum saw a red and blue and yellow coat so . . .

Josie went to school in her new coat and . . .

Name

Put the sentences in the right order.

"That was scary!" said Toad.

ting-a-ling, ting-a-ling

"That was very scary!" said Toad.

"Look out!" said Frog. "It's a bicycle!"

Toad crawled on to the road.

Vroom! Vroom!

The bicycle zoomed down the road.

"Look out!" said Frog. "It's a car!"

The car zoomed down the road.

Name

Write your own story ending.
What do Frog and Toad say?

Vroom!

Skill: writing story ending

© Harcourt Education Ltd, 2007

Name

Colour the rhyming words green.
Colour the capital letters red.
Colour the compound words yellow.

Old Mrs Mog has twenty-six cats,
and twenty-six cats has she.
Wherever you look in Mrs Mog's house,
a cat is sure to be.

There are cats in the bathroom,
and cats in the bed.
Cats in the kitchen,
and cats being fed.

There are cats by the beehive,
chasing the bees.
There are cats on the rooftops,
and cats in the trees.

Mrs Mog's Cats

Skill: identifying rhyming words, capital letters
and compound words

RIGBY
star

What do you think Mrs Mog says?
Fill in the speech bubble.

Name

Write in the characters' names. Sequence the characters in the order they appear in the story. Match the words to the character.

_____
_____

_____
_____

_____
_____

_____
_____

_____
_____

"He's just in here."

"Pock! Pock!"

"Quack! Quack!"

"Quick!"

"Hiss! Hiss!"

Name

Write your own story ending.
What happened next?

_____

_____

_____

_____

_____

_____

Chicken Licken
Skill: composing own writing

Name

Put the ingredients and instructions for Blue Goo in the right order.

What you need:

 a dollop of durble dribble

 some slippery slubber shoots

 one glass of gunky glue

 a frilly frottle's feather

 one jug of jiggle jelly

What you do:

Cover and cook.

Dish up.

Sniff and sample.

Simmer and stir.

★★★ **Blue Goo**

Skill: story recall and sequencing instructions

Name
....

Write a recipe for your own monster stew.

What you need:

_____   _____

_____   _____

What you do:

1 _____

2 _____

3 _____

4 _____

Draw a picture of your monster stew.

Name

Cut out these words and play snap with them. Snap the words which contain the phoneme 'ee'.

creeping	along	see	caterpillar
tree	lovely	honey	three
comes	hiding	sweet	singing
peeping	song	bee	runny
curly	tea	what	hive
along	hungry	look	clever

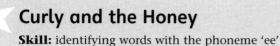

Curly and the Honey

Skill: identifying words with the phoneme 'ee'

Write a 'Thank you' letter to Curly for the honey, from one of his friends.

Thank you

Dear Curly,

Love from

Circle the words with the 'oe' phoneme, as in the word 'old'. Underline the words with the 'ae' phoneme, as in the word 'away'.

An (old) man had a <u>lazy</u> son.

So he told his son,

"This map shows there is gold in that field."

The son jumped up right away.

He dug in the sunshine . . . and in the rain.

He dug up weeds and stones.

But he did not dig up the gold!

Name ....

Write in the speech bubbles what the characters say.

Put the two parts of the sentence together.
Match the picture to the sentence.

Snow boots are for	listening in lessons.
Lace-ups are for	building an igloo.
Slippers are for	playing the princess.
Party shoes are for	snuggling with Snowy and snacking on the sofa.

Super-Duper Shoes

Skill: making sentences

GLUE

RIGBY
star

© Harcourt Education Ltd, 2007

Talk to a friend about your favourite shoes.
Draw a picture of them and write about them.

What sort of shoes are they?

_____

What are they for?

_____

_____

Why do you like them?

_____

_____

_____

_____

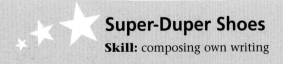

Name ....

Circle the words with the phoneme 'ow' as in the word 'down'.

High on the (mountain) top, the Storm Bird pounded its powerful wings and the ground shook.

A great shower of rain fell.

The rain washed the whale out of the well.

"Goodness, look at those cliffs!" said the whale.

"It's a town," giggled the frog.

The Whale in the Well

Skill: identifying the phoneme 'ow' in a variety of representations

© Harcourt Education Ltd, 2007

Name

Write what the whale sees next in the wonderful new world. Draw a picture.

Complete the sentences using the
right word.

sing	sleep	hear	cry
singing	sleeping	hearing	crying

George the Giant loved to _____ .

"We'll be able to _____ at night,"
said the mums and dads.

"We'll be able to _____ the television,"
said the brothers and sisters.

"Please stop _____ , and go to sleep,"
said everyone.

"The babies didn't _____ when George
was singing."

"Please start _____ again," said the people.

The Singing Giant
Skill: using grammatical awareness to complete sentences

Write what you think they are saying.

George: " _____

_____ "

Grandmas and grandpas: " _____

_____ "

Sisters and brothers:" _____

_____ "

Babies: " _____

_____ "

Match the words to the characters in Scene Three.

We have come to tell you to stop singing.	Hello, everyone. Nice to see you. Have you come to hear me sing?
You must stop singing, George.	And I can't hear the television because of all the noise.
But I love to sing. Ohhhh. Sniffle, sniffle.	We are now at George's house again.
No, we have not!	Yes, I can't sleep because of all the noise.

Fill in this chart.

Title: The Singing Giant – A Play
Author: Illustrator: Characters:
Scene 1 takes place in George the Giant's house. Scene 2 takes place _____ Scene 3 _____ Scene 4 _____ Scene 5 _____ Scene 6 _____
The play is about . . .

Name

READING ★ FICTION

3.1

GREEN LEVEL

Put the two parts of each sentence together.

She ran away	as she could.
as fast as he could.	The fox jumped up
than I am.	The fox ran away
I can shout much louder	as fast as she could.
into the sky.	The fox is faster and stronger
She cheeped as loudly	than you can.

Clever Chick

Skill: making sentences, recognising capital letters and full stops

RIGBY **star**

© Harcourt Education Ltd, 2007

Name

Describe the chick and the fox.

I'm _____

_____

I'm _____

_____

Clever Chick

Skill: describing characters

RIGBY
star ★

Complete the crossword.

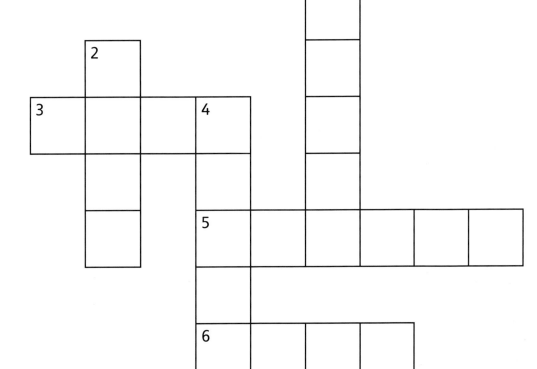

Clues

Across

3. Josie _____ on holiday.

5. Josie and Ravi liked _____ the horses.

6. "We're too tired," said the two _____ .

Down

1. Josie's Dad _____ very fast.

2. "We did but we're _____ tired," said Josie and Ravi.

4. "I'm _____!" said Josie.

Name

Write what they did on holiday.

Josie's Holiday Diary

On the first day,

On the second day,

On the third day,

Name

Complete the crossword.

Clues
Across
1. On _____ we painted yo-yo pictures.
3. Mr Rust _____ yo-yos.
5. On _____ we did yo-yo maths.
7. "Wow! We're _____!" we said.

Down
1. On _____ we read yo-yo books.
2. On Wednesday, we _____ stories.
4. On _____, we hated yo-yos.
6. We took our _____ home.

Name

···

Write a class diary.

On Monday, _____

_____

_____

On Tuesday, _____

_____

_____

On Wednesday, _____

_____

_____

On Thursday, _____

_____

_____

On Friday, _____

_____

_____

Yo-Yo a Go-Go

Skill: retelling a story in diary format

Complete the crossword.

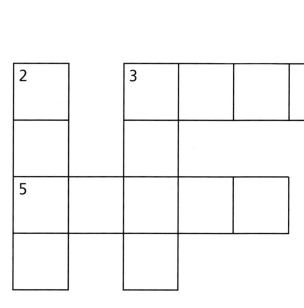

Clues

Across

3. "I can make soup from this _____ ."

4. "Can we _____ the soup now?"

5. "Then I put in this small, _____ stone."

Down

1. "If I had some potatoes it would taste _____ ."

2. On his _____, he had a big pot of water.

3. After a while the man tasted the _____ .

Name

Retell the story.

 Once upon a time _____

_____

_____

 One day, _____

_____

 First _____

_____

_____

 Then _____

_____

_____

 Soon _____

_____

Then _____

_____

★★★ **Stone Soup**

Skill: retelling story with story language

Put the sentences in the right order.

The man felt the wind on his back.

He pulled his coat to him.

There was a man walking across a field.

Then the man took off his coat!

"I am stronger than you," said the smiling sun.

He pushed back his coat.

The man felt the sun on his back.

The wind was so angry he blew away to sea.

One day, the wind and the sun had a contest.

The Wind and the Sun
Skill: sequencing

RIGBY
star ★

Name

Write how the man would retell the story.

One day, I was walking across a field . . .

Then the wind stopped . . .

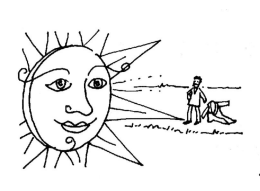

The sun felt very strong . . .

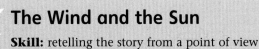

Put the two parts of each sentence together.

"It's as big as	in Grandma's garden.
The pumpkin was a	a house!" they said.
Dan planted the seed	little bigger.
Then one day the pumpkin	playhouse!" said Dan.
my bicycle," said Dan.	stopped growing.
"It's as big as	came to see it.
"It's as big as	"It's a fantastic
my football," said Dan.	Some people from television

Name

Write what Grandma told the television people.

The Fantastic Pumpkin

Skill: retelling story from point of view

Name

Circle the words with the 'au' phoneme as in the word 'for'.

In the morning, Josie took Popcorn into

the garden.

She showed him how to run after a ball

and bring it back.

She took him out into the street.

She taught him how to walk by her side

and how to sit at the kerb.

Josie and the Puppy

Skill: identifying the phoneme 'au' in a variety of representations

© Harcourt Education Ltd, 2007

How did Josie look after Popcorn?
Write a list of the things she needed:

_____   _____

_____   _____

_____   _____

Write what she did:

_____

_____

_____

_____

_____

_____

_____

Josie and the Puppy

Skill: writing lists and instructions

Name

....

Read each sentence, then circle Yes or No.

Elvis crashed into a planet.   Yes   No

Elvis was happy when he got out of
the spaceship.   Yes   No

Elvis met a big, hairy creature.   Yes   No

The big hairy creature was angry with Elvis. Yes   No

The creature gave Elvis some food.   Yes   No

Elvis did not want to go home.   Yes   No

The creature mended the spaceship.   Yes   No

Elvis and the creature were friends.   Yes   No

Fill in the missing words.

| clearly | cheerfully | nearer | feast | cleared |
| tear | peered | creature | here | year |

He couldn't see _____.

"Where am I?" he said as he _____ around.

The sound came _____ and _____.

Just then, the fog _____ and Elvis saw a giant hairy _____.

"What a _____!" he said _____.

"I will never be able to go home," sighed Elvis, and he wiped away a _____.

"It is ages since we had a tourist _____," said the _____.

"Will you come back next _____?"

Match the sentences to the characters.

There is going to be a party in the South!

Guess what?

There is going to be a party in the North!

There would be lots of food!

There is going to be a party in the West!

Good news!

There is going to be a party in the East!

Come on!

That way he would not miss a thing.

Big Spider

Skill: matching speech to characters

Name

3.2

WRITING ★ PHONICS

GREEN LEVEL

Find out about spiders and write a report. Draw a picture of a spider.

What do spiders look like?

_____

_____

_____

Where do they live?

_____

_____

_____

_____

★ ★ ★ **Big Spider**

Skill: writing a non-chronological report

RIGBY star

© Harcourt Education Ltd, 2007

Name

Read the sentences and put them into the right order.

The farmer, the fisherman and the woman left in a hurry.

"A talking yam!" said the Chief. "What nonsense!"

"Now stop wasting my time before I throw you all in jail."

"Quite right," said his chair.

One day a farmer was digging his field.

They went to tell the Chief.

The farmer was so amazed that he ran away down the hill.

"How can that be true? That is not possible,"
said the fisherman.

The fisherman was so amazed that he ran after the farmer.

A woman was swimming down the river.

Too Much Talk

Skill: story recall and sequencing

RIGBY
star

Write what happens after the end
of the story.

The Chief was so amazed that

_____

_____

_____

_____

_____

_____

_____

Name

Circle Yes or No

A lizard's ears are on its neck.

Yes   No

A frog's ears are on its feelers.

Yes   No

A mosquito's ears are on its body.

Yes   No

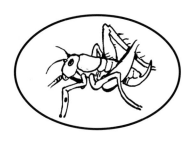

A cricket's ears are on its legs.

Yes   No

Where are your ears?

My ears are _____.

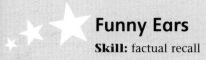

Funny Ears

Skill: factual recall

Complete the sentences and the labels.

ears

An ostrich's ears
are on its head.

A lizard's ears
_____ ___ _____ neck.

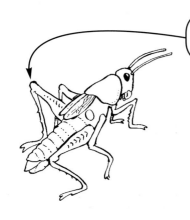

A grasshopper's ears
_____ ___ _____ body.

Name

Complete the chart.

	kitten	pup	calf
baby cat	✓		
baby elephant			
baby whale			
baby rabbit			
baby seal			
baby cow			
baby dog			

Name

··

Complete the sentences and the labels.

kitten

This is a **baby cat.**
It is **called** a **kitten.**

pup

_____ __ __ **baby seal.**
__ __ **called** __ **pup.**

_____ __ __ **baby cow.**
__ __ **called** __ **calf.**

Name ....

Cut out the captions at the bottom of the page and match them to the pictures.

| The pine cones fall to the ground. | The sapling grows and grows. | The seedling grows and grows. |

| A pine tree grows in the forest. | The seeds from the pine cones go into the ground. |

From Seedling to Tree

Skill: sequencing

RIGBY
star

Fill in the missing words about how a tadpole changes into a frog.

(front legs) (frog) (eats)

(smaller) (back legs)

 The tadpole eats and _____ .

 The tadpole grows two _____ .

 The tadpole grows two _____ .

 The tadpole's tail gets smaller
and _____ .

 The tadpole is now a _____ .

Look at the pictures and read the sentences. Tick ✔ the sentences which are right. Put a cross ✘ by the sentences which are wrong.

1   This is a toy today.   ☐

2   These houses are from long ago. ☐

3   These are clothes today.   ☐

4   This is a car from long ago.   ☐

5   This is a classroom today.   ☐

 This is a **house** today.

 This is a **house** from long ago.

Complete the sentences.

 This is a _____ car _____.

 _____ car _____.

 _____ toy _____.

_____ toy _____.

_____ hat _____.

_____ hat _____.

Today and Long Ago
Skill: writing captions

RIGBY
star

Complete the chart.

What It's Made Of

	wood	paper	glass	metal	plastic	wool
jars						
hard hat						
keys						
tissues						
socks						
chair						

Name

Complete the captions.

This **trumpet** is made of **metal.**

_____ **puppet** __ _____ __ **wool.**

_____ **book** __ _____ __ **paper.**

READING ★ NON-FICTION
2.1
BLUE LEVEL

Complete the pictures.

KEY	likes	doesn't like	doesn't like very much

My dog
likes water.

My dog
likes food.

My dog
likes a walk.

My dog
likes to run.

My dog
doesn't like
his bath.

My dog
doesn't like
being dried
very much.

I love my dog and
my dog loves me!

I Take Care of My Dog
Skill: comprehension

RIGBY
star

Name

....

Write the questions. Add the ?

Do dogs need water every day
Yes. Dogs need water every day.

_____?
Yes. Dogs need food every day.

_____
Yes. Dogs need exercise every day.

_____
No. Dogs do not need a bath
every day.

I Take Care of My Dog

Skill: writing questions, using question marks

RIGBY
star

Play the board game with a partner. Take turns to roll a dice. Who can get to the finish first?

Joe's trip to London board game

17	**18** Tower Bridge Joe saw boats go under the bridge. Go on one space.	**19**	**20** Finish
16	**15**	**14** Tower of London Joe liked the cannons. Go on two spaces.	**13**
9	**10** The Houses of Parliament Joe wanted to look at the river. Go back two spaces.	**11**	**12** St Paul's Cathedral Joe went inside to look at the dome. Go back one space.
8	**7**	**6** Oxford St Joe missed the bus. Miss a turn.	**5**
1 Start	**2** London Eye Joe could see all of London. Go on three spaces.	**3**	**4**

Where is Joe?
Skill: comprehension

Joe bought a postcard in London to send to his grandma. Draw a picture for the front of the postcard, and write what Joe wrote to his grandma on the back.

front

back

Mrs Little,

3 School Road,

Bradcroft

★★★
Where is Joe?
Skill: writing a postcard

RIGBY
star

© Harcourt Education Ltd, 2007

Name

Here are the instructions for making a monster mask. They are not in the right order. Write a number in the boxes to put them in the right order.

Make your own monster mask
You will need:

a paper plate

paint

wool

scissors

glue

Stick the wool onto the plate.

Paint the paper plate.

Cut the wool to make hair.

Cut out holes for the eyes.

 ★★★

Make Your Own Monster!
Skill: sequencing

RIGBY
star ★

© Harcourt Education Ltd, 2007

Name ....

Fill in the missing words for making a train.

Make your own train
You will need:

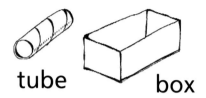
tube   box

a paper plate   paint   scissors   glue

1 Glue the _____ to the top of the box.

2 Cut four circles out of the paper plate to make _____.

3 Glue the wheels on the _____.

4 Now _____ the train.

| paint | tube | wheels | box |

Name

Join the sentences.

 An ape uses its feet   to hang upside down.

 A badger uses its feet   to climb.

 A bat uses its feet   to dig.

 A blackbird uses its feet   to swim.

 A turtle uses its feet   to catch fish.

 An eagle uses its feet   to perch.

Animal Feet

Skill: comprehension

Use the words to write the labels.

> ape • talons • badger • tree • fish
> • eagle • claws • ground • feet

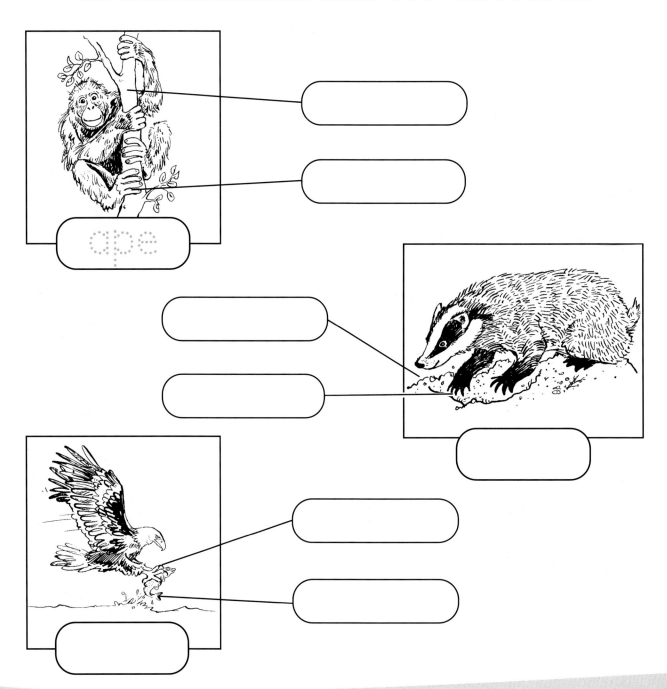

Put the sentences in the right order.

Put peanut butter on the pine cone.

Cut the string.

Roll the pine cone in the birdseed.

Tie the string to the pine cone.

Tie the bird feeder to a tree.

How to make a Bird Feeder
Skill: sequencing

RIGBY star

© Harcourt Education Ltd, 2007

Name
....

Complete the instructions.

How to make a Bird Feeder

What you need:

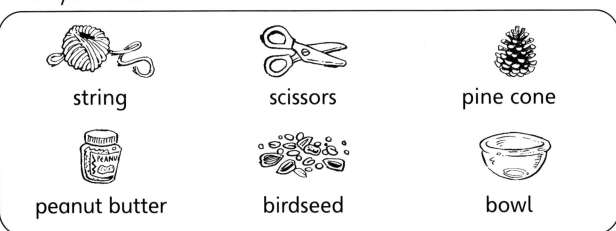

string	scissors	pine cone
peanut butter	birdseed	bowl

1. Cut _____ _____.

2. Tie the _____ to the

   _____ _____.

3. Put _____ _____ on

   the _____ _____.

4. Put the _____ in a big _____.

5. Roll the _____ _____ in the _____.

6. Tie the _____ _____ to a tree.

How to make a Bird Feeder
Skill: using the language of instructions

Read the captions. Draw a picture for each one.

We pitched the tent.

Dad cooked the food outside.

We went to sleep in the tent.

Name

Write about a trip you have been on.

My trip

Where did you go?

_____

Who did you go with?

_____

What did you take?

_____

What did you see?

_____

What did you do?

_____

How good was your trip? Tick a box.

☹ It was OK.   ☐
☺ It was good.   ☐
☺ It was fantastic!   ☐

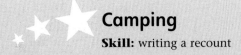
★★★ **Camping**
Skill: writing a recount

RIGBY
star ★

Answer the questions.

How Does Water Change?

Contents

George Huxley

R RIGBY

On which page is there information about solids?

Which page is the introduction on?

If you want to read about gases where will you look?

Which page is the index on?

If you want to read about liquids where will you look?

★ ★ ★ **How Does Water Change?**
Skill: using a contents page

RIGBY
star ★

© Harcourt Education Ltd, 2007

Are the things below a liquid, a solid or a gas? Write a sentence for each one.

 Milk is a liquid.
_____

  Chocolate _____

 Butter _____

 Steam _____

 Tomato sauce _____

 Snow _____

Index of Photocopy Masters

A code of F/Ph/NF is used to indicate whether each photocopy master is related to a fiction, fiction with a phonic focus, or non-fiction book.

Level	Photocopy Master	
	Reading	Writing
Fiction		
Yellow Level		
Josie and the Baby	F1.1	F1.2
Pop! A Play	F2.1	F2.2
Grandpa	F3.1	F3.2
What a Week!	F4.1	F4.2
At Last!	F5.1	F5.2
The Computer Game	F6.1	F6.2
Where is Curly?	F7.1	F7.2
Have you Got everything, Colin?	F8.1	F8.2
The Lion's Dinner	F9.1	F9.2
The Dentist	F10.1	F10.2
Super Shopping	F11.1	F11.2
Where's Our Car?	F12.1	F12.2
I Can't Open It!	F13.1	F13.2
Curly to the Rescue	F14.1	F14.2
Rush Hour	F15.1	F15.2
Be Quiet!	F16.1	F16.2
Josie Helps Out	Ph1.1	Ph1.2
Ping-Pong	Ph2.1	Ph2.2
Booooo!	Ph3.1	Ph3.2
Bert's Boat	Ph4.1	Ph4.2
Blue Level		
A Ball Called Sam	F1.1	F1.2
Josie and the Play	F2.1	F2.2
Terrible Tiger	F3.1	F3.2
Space Ant	F4.1	F4.2
Bully Bear	F5.1	F5.2
Josie's New Coat	F6.1	F6.2
Vroom!	F7.1	F7.2
Mrs Mog's Cats	F8.1	F8.2

Level	Photocopy Master	
Blue Level continued	*Reading*	*Writing*
Chicken Licken	Ph1.1	Ph1.2
Blue Goo	Ph2.1	Ph2.2
Curly and the Honey	Ph3.1	Ph3.2
Field of Gold	Ph4.1	Ph4.2
Super-Duper Shoes	Ph5.1	Ph5.2
The Whale in the Well	Ph6.1	Ph6.2
Green Level		
The Singing Giant (story)	F1.1	F1.2
The Singing Giant (play)	F2.1	F2.2
Clever Chick	F3.1	F3.2
Josie Goes on Holiday	F4.1	F4.2
Yo-yo a Go-go	F5.1	F5.2
Stone Soup	F6.1	F6.2
The Wind and the Sun	F7.1	F7.2
The Fantastic Pumpkin	F8.1	F8.2
Josie and the Puppy	Ph1.1	Ph1.2
Elvis and the Space Junk	Ph2.1	Ph2.2
Big Spider	Ph3.1	Ph3.2
Too Much Talk	Ph4.1	Ph4.2

Non-fiction		
Yellow Level		
Funny Ears	NF1.1	NF1.2
Baby Animals	NF2.1	NF2.2
From Seedling to Tree	NF3.1	NF3.2
Today and Long Ago	NF4.1	NF4.2
Blue Level		
What's It Made of?	NF1.1	NF1.2
I Take Care of My Dog	NF2.1	NF2.2
Where Is Joe?	NF3.1	NF3.2
Make Your Own Monster!	NF4.1	NF4.2
Green Level		
Animal Feet	NF1.1	NF1.2
How to Make a Bird Feeder	NF2.1	NF2.2
Camping	NF3.1	NF3.2
How Does Water Change?	NF4.1	NF4.2

RIGBY star